God to Malaria
Communications from the
Spirit World

THE GLASGOW ASSOCIATION OF SPIRITUALISTS

To all the brave pioneers of Spiritualism.

CONTENTS

ACKNOWLEDGEMENTS

Special thanks to

Dr Allan Scott MBChB DTM&H DObst RCOG
Jacqui McGleish OSNU
Wendy Lyon OSNU
Joanne Ward CSNU(t)

INTRODUCTION

During the early 1990s, when I was a serving police officer with Strathclyde Police, I took an interest in Spiritualism. Don't ask me why. It was just one of those things. I started attending services at the Glasgow Association of Spiritualists. Quite often, my dad, who was *physically* alive at that time, would accompany me, not because he was a Spiritualist (he wasn't), but because it was a day out, and stopped my mother complaining that he was getting under her feet.

Dad had Parkinson's disease which affected him terribly. He was a retired medical doctor, and had spent the final part of his working years in general practice in Kent. He did, however, have a very good knowledge of tropical medicine, having lived seven years in Assam, India, caring for the workforces on a number of different tea gardens during the 1950s. But he hadn't just treated his patients, he'd also researched into different methods of malaria control, documenting his findings in published papers, and commenting on them in a series of letters he wrote to his parents during his time in India. He died in 2004, aged eighty.

My partner, David, most certainly was *not* a Spiritualist, and was far from open to the idea that consciousness just might survive physical death. He was a Scottish scientist, who had spent time in the military in America. His disinterest in Spiritualism was so profound, it even stopped me from attending services at the Church.

However, when he quite unexpectedly died from a heart attack in February 2013, things started to change.

I moved in with my mother, and spent months reorganising things, much of which is a blur, although I do recall the sense that I was able to do more than I ever thought I could, and was convinced that *someone,* or, *something* was behind this. I reattended the services at the Glasgow Association of Spiritualists, and for the first number of weeks received constant 'messages' from my father and, believe it or not, David.

They described David's death. I'd been away at the time, and had discovered David's body the following day, stiff and upright on the couch in the sitting room. David told me he'd passed very quickly. One minute he was in the physical world, and the next, he was somewhere else, and very confused. He said his father had come to meet him, and expressed his amazement that his consciousness was still alive. Furthermore, he wanted me to pursue my interest in Spiritualism, something he would never have said as a physical human being. And that might have been that, only not so, for it was during this period that strange things began to happen.

I awoke one night, and became conscious of small black spots dotted around my bedroom. They were clearly visible against the white furniture. For some reason, I didn't pay too much attention to them, and might have confused them with dreams. Over time, they continued to appear, until larger flat spots, similar to tar in colour, began to emerge. These would move around, and manifest on the white ceiling, as well as the white furniture. Some even began shooting through the air and across the light-coloured carpet, towards the bed where I lay. Some remained black, and some turned grey. Some grew big, and some remained small. Some even grew legs, resembling spiders.

I decided to search the Internet to try and find some answers, but when I read that such experiences were no more than night-time terrors due to psychiatric issues (and required medical attention), I begged to differ. The incidents were no longer frightening me, and I do not believe I am psychotic. If I am, then, as will be observed later, so are the cameras in my three mobile phones.

I continued to wake up within a tank of interesting activity. The spots, whatever their size and colour, started to emerge in a grey haze, some moving at incredible speed. It was then I decided to interact with them. As a spot would approach, I would raise my hand and watch it examine my fingers. At the start, the spot would sometimes move round the shape of my fingers, and other times, I would feel a tingle, or nothing at all. On one occasion, I touched a spot with the tip of my right index finger, and felt an electrical charge zoom down my arm. Then things began to develop further.

As I would lie half-awake in bed, my eyes shut, images, preceded by a flickering sensation and a swoosh in my head, were actually beginning to appear inside my head. Colourful pictures, resembling Pop Art and vintage posters, popped into my head, followed by indecipherable flashes of writing and table charts, none of which I could read, moving at great speed, as if being processed by a computer.

Was this the type of thing the mediums at the Church experienced? Was this some kind of connection with the Spirit World? My head was spinning.

In January 2015, I began to attend workshops and development circles at the Church. The medium in charge was Jacqui McGleish. However, despite all the activities going on at home, my experiences during these sessions consisted mainly of merging patterns of black and purple, decorated with sparkles, and, if I was lucky, the odd tadpole. I was also attending meetings at the SSPR (Scottish Society for Psychical Research), so taking the bull by the horns, I spoke briefly to someone there about my experiences. Since I had no witnesses, the person suggested I take photographs. I did, and managed to capture some very interesting things with the cameras in my Nokia, Alcatel and Motorola mobile phones.

So, what now? Simple, really: it was time for a private sitting.

On 8 October 2015 I sat with Jacqui. Dad and David came through, and both confirmed their presence in my room at night. I began to converse with them (through Jacqui, of course), and when I referred to the letters Dad had written in India, he indicated that the things manifesting around me had something to do with them. He would not explain further, but what he did say was that I had to read more, and stop missing windows of opportunity as I had done in the past.

So, where was I?

Spots and spiders? Indecipherable words and charts? Photographs of things the camera could see, which my naked eye could *not*. First with my old Nokia phone, then an Alcatel and also a nice new Motorola. Three cameras, all picking up something. Heck: even the microwave dial was going the wrong way.

It was time to explore further, which is exactly what I did.

Caroline A Scott
President
The Glasgow Association of Spiritualists
August, 2024

1

PHOTOGRAPHS AND DRAWINGS

On Monday 12 December 2016, I prepared myself for another interview. My photos, which were in colour, were on my laptop, my questions were prepared, so all I needed now was to have the confidence to discuss my evidence with a medium, and hopefully get some input from the Spirit World. As a police officer I'd been told to keep an open mind, and since this was an investigation, I would do exactly that.

I arrived at Jacqui's, nervous but keen. I downed a cup of tea, then it was onward march to the room of reckoning. I turned on my laptop, produced my notes and watched as Jacqui, quite indiscernibly, went into action. If I'd expected a dramatic change, there was none. She simply tuned in and waited for me.

I went to the first photo, and switching on my recording device (Motorola mobile phone), nervously began. I told her that I'd managed to capture photographs that appeared to contain orbs, distortions and ectoplasm, and wanted my father to explain what was happening. Dad proved keen to comply, and came through quite promptly. He confirmed that deceased members of my family had been present at the time the photos were taken, (including himself and David). Their energies had caused the distortions as a way of proving their presence in and around my home. There then ensued an interesting dialogue.

(It should be noted that the photos have been reproduced in black and white for better clarity.)

C = Caroline
J = Jacqui

Nokia Mobile Phone

Photo 1

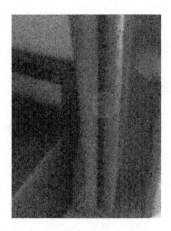

C: This one seems to show a couple of orbs on the curtains and quite a lot of distortion around the curtains themselves, and also the bench: it's a plastic bench in the bedroom. I'm wondering if my father's able to come forward and give some information on that.

J: I actually think there's someone standing there. There's another orb there. It looks as if somebody's there, or somebody's trying to come through there. Is that near where your dad would sit?

C: This is the bedroom he had. I restructured the room and moved his desk there. It was the bedroom that both my parents used. My mum moved into the little bedroom because I needed the big bedroom for the Internet.

J: Right. OK.

C: So, it was his room, and it was his side of the bed.

J: Right. Because I feel as if I would have sat there. I would have looked out in that area. But there is something else there. There's definitely something else. Down the right side of the picture in front of the big orb at the top. There's actually something there. You can see it.

C: That's very interesting. Does Dad have a comment?

J: I don't think it's your dad. I think he would have sat in that room, but I don't think that's your dad trying to come through. I think it's someone else. Did your dad have a brother?

C: Yes.

J: I think that could be your dad's brother.

Photo 2

J: That picture's quite interesting. I actually think wherever that picture has been taken, somebody is sending healing. And actually, it looks like a Paisley pattern. You don't know if someone lived in Paisley?

C: Me and David.

J: There's a Paisley pattern in that. Do you see that?

C: Yes. And I've noticed there's something up here, up at the top.

J: Yes. It's funny the way that that actually looks. That pattern. Did somebody used to keep birds?

C: David kept birds.

J: Right. OK. There's a bird in there. Look. The tail of the bird. There's the head and the tail. There. Do you see it?

C: Yes. That picture is actually the back of a brown chair.

J: Really?

C: A brown plastic chair that I had in my room. It's now in the dining room for my sister to use. It's an office chair: big and very dark brown. Plastic back.

Photo 3

C: This is my dressing table, and if you look up here, it's like a face.

J: Yes. Definitely.

C: The top right-hand corner. Do Dad and David have a comment?

J: I actually think that's David in the room. He's trying to let you know that he's there. I think he's there quite a lot. I'm just trying to see if there's anything else in the picture. I think there's an arm here coming out, so I don't know whether they're reaching across; you don't keep your jewellery there?

C: Yes. That's a box with jewellery in it.

J: Is his ring in there? Something connected to him in there?

C: I'll tell you what's there. On the other side of it is the box with his ashes. I didn't see that face to begin with, but it was looking out the picture. It seems like a face laughing at me.

J: Yes. Definitely. Because it's a build-up of ectoplasm, you won't necessarily see it as a 'face' face; it's got to mould and you might have caught it halfway between that.

C: It's more like a cartoon face, isn't it?

J: Yes.

C: It's like a 'monkey' face!

J: Yes.

Photo 4

J: Oh yes. Look at that.

C: And we've got three funny circles.

J: They're definitely orbs. You can definitely see that there are orbs there. And again, it's energy. There's definitely energy in the room. The first orb at the top there looks as if there's something trying to build up within it.

C: It looks as if there's a mouth and eyes.

J: Yes. I would have said that too. Actually, there's a shadow underneath it. There's a bigger orb, and then another orb there. See them: one, two, three. So, again, it looks as if they could be just trying to build up. And that's in the same room?

C: It's all in my bedroom. Again, it's that same chair.

J: Does your mum ever say she feels anything?

C: Oh yes, but she puts it down to something else. She sees little men and smoke on the curtains. She puts it down to her eyesight (macular degeneration). She doesn't know I've got all this because it would freak her out.

J: Yes. I would understand that. This isn't something that 'normal' people understand: well, I don't mean it that way, but you know what I mean.

Photo 5

C: This is my dad's little bathroom. Is that his face there?

J: That's not your dad. No, that's your Aunty Mary!

C: Is it? Aunty Mary? What's she doing in my dad's bathroom?

J: I don't know!

C: Do you want to ask her?

J: I actually think she's just pottering about. But that is definitely your Aunty Mary. And actually, you can see there's all different ones coming here. I think she's just about the house.

C: She probably is.

J: That *is* your Aunty Mary, and she doesn't feel very tall.

C: No. She's not tall.

J: But that's definitely her. She's quite nosey. She likes to know what's going on. I think that's why she's popping in. Just to be nosey. That's definitely your Aunty Mary.

Alcatel Mobile Phone

Photo 6

C: Now, I'm going to the Alcatel phone. (It's dark outside.) The light (electric) is coming in from the hall. It's shining into the little toilet there. It looks like black mist there.

J: It does. It definitely looks like it, but it's going across as well. So, you can definitely see that.

C: Again, it's a different camera from the Nokia. This is the Alcatel. Is it ectoplasm?

J: Yes. And I actually think you've maybe just got a house full of energy; and they're using it to come forward. But I don't think that's any of the others; I don't think that's your dad or David; and I don't think it's your Aunty Mary. Who's William?

C: That's my uncle. My dad's brother. Uncle Willie.

J: And he's in spirit?

C: Yes. In fact, there are two Uncle Willies. My mum's got a brother as well.

J: I think you've got William in there as well.

C: There's the two.

J: Was one tall?

C: Yes. The other one (my mum's brother) was very small.

J: It's the tall one. You're kind of allowing them all in. They're all coming. I think you're like a light bulb and they're like moths drawn in to the light. Which is nice.

Motorola Mobile Phone

Photo 7

C: (*Photo shows the top of my bedside cabinet*) Is that my dad?

J: I think it's your dad, yes.

C: What does he say?

J: He comes around your room because he knows you're more susceptible than your mum. So, he comes to keep an eye on you, and see what's what. Your dad also likes to talk.

C: I do things. I get ideas.

J: I think it's your dad. Yes. I think he's trying to give you ideas. He's trying to talk to you and tell you, so you know.

Interesting and very comforting. My next step was to show Jacqui a selection of drawings I had made of 'things' I'd seen with my own eyes on waking up in my room during the early hours. Jacqui confirmed that my dad was responsible.

Drawing 1

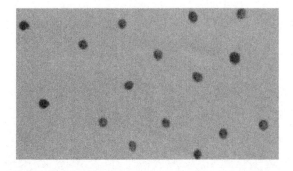

(Small spots on my white furniture and in the air.)

Drawing 2

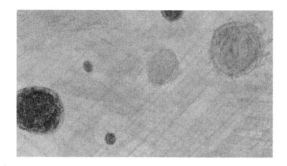

(*Different sized spots in quivering, hazy grey ectoplasm in the air.*)

Drawing 3

(*On the ceiling: lights were like sparkles from a firework sparkler.*)

J: I think that's definitely your dad.

C: Can you ask him if it's because when I'm waking up, I'm more susceptible to 'seeing' these things?

J: He's trying to use your energy. And I think he wakes you up. I think you sense him there and that's why you wake up.

So here was the thing. The sceptic could quite easily say that the spots were simply figments of my imagination. Where was my proof? Well, as far as I was concerned, I had found the proof! Not only had my three cameras picked up different anomalies, my Nokia had actually captured a spot!

C: This is interesting. You can see the black spot there.

J: Yes.

C: Now, the spot of light came from outside. It was the way the curtain was positioned. I could see *that* with the naked eye, so I wondered if there was anything else there. That's when I saw the little black spot through the Nokia phone.

J: Yes.

C: So, that's the first time I've managed to photograph a black spot!

J: There's another one, down there.

C: These spots are interesting. These are the things I wake up and see.

J: But that might be (this is going to sound really bizarre) that could be an orb before the ectoplasm kicks in.

C: OK.

J: So, what you're seeing is the beginning of a build-up, and then you get an orb as in an energy orb. I reckon that's what you're getting. Is that your bedroom?

C: No. That's the sitting room. But it's over in the corner where my dad would have sat.

J: Right.

But it didn't end with spots: **Drawings 4 and 5**.

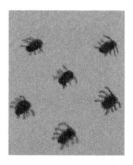

C: Who brought the spiders?

J: That's your dad as well. But I think it's the same thing. It's just maybe you 'see' it differently; or your eyes 'see' it differently. You're seeing them as spiders.

Then there was the Union Jack. I'd awoken early one morning to find it quivering, inches from my nose: **Drawing 6.**

C: This was just before the referendum (Scottish Independence). Is this my dad?

J: Yes. Definitely your dad.

C: Can you ask him what the Union Jack was about?

J: Did your dad vote Conservative?

C: Yes.

J: He just said: 'Conservative.' I think it's just your dad's way of letting you know it's him.

C: So, these are the things I see externally when I'm waking up. I've also seen things internally on waking up when my eyes are still shut: even a firework display that swooshed inside my head. When I meditate, I sometimes see black spots or tadpoles.

J: That's birth. The tadpoles are birth. So, it's the birth of something. And again, it's grabbing hold of it. I actually think the fireworks are where they're letting you know it's starting to happen. Or, that it's starting to work for you.

2

THE START OF SOMETHING

Well, there you had it: straight from the horse's mouth. Only Dad was clearly in the driving seat. He'd spoken of birth and grabbing hold of something. But grabbing hold of what? Fortunately, the fireworks in my head seemed to be a good sign, even though I had to keep reminding myself that if I *was* 'going off my head', then so too were my mobile phones.

The strange thing was that none of these activities had actually happened until after David's death, so, in all probability, David's death had been the trigger. But what was Dad wanting me to do? He'd brought in family members, and I'd discovered they were as curious as I was, with one exception: they had already been here at one point in their lives. They knew earth for what it was: the nice bits, and the not so nice bits. But what did I know about the Spirit World? Very little.

So, here was the thing. I was becoming aware of very strange phenomena; therefore, if Dad was able to communicate all these things to me, then that had to mean one thing: consciousness, or whatever it is that makes us think, has to survive the death of the physical body.

I'd already been given proof during services at the Glasgow Association of Spiritualists, but these personal experiences were literally bringing things closer to home, and adding more meaning. The photos and drawings had been explained, but somehow that wasn't enough. I wanted to know more about what happens in the Spirit World. In fact, I wanted to know *everything* that happens in the Spirit World, as unrealistic as that might actually be. I also wanted to know how the physical earth really began, and how it continues to function with particular regard to its interpenetration with the Spirit World.

As daunting and enterprising as that might seem, I wasn't put off, even though I wasn't really off to a good start. Albeit I had O-levels in Physics, Chemistry, Biology and Maths, I had last studied these subjects, way back in the mid-seventies. There was a lot of research to do, so I rolled up my sleeves and began to dig.

The Glasgow Association of Spiritualists is one of the many Spiritualist churches affiliated to the Spiritualists' National Union (SNU), which provides guidance for those running the different churches. I'd attended enough services to know that each individual communicating spirit (communicator) is what is left of an individual human being, following physical death. I'd further discovered that Spiritualist churches operate on the basis of the Seven Principles, passed on by one Robert Owen, through the mediumship of one Emma Hardinge Britten, in the nineteenth century.

I immersed myself in books: but so many ideas, and so many opinions. Although Spiritualism is a recognised religion, the subject is definitely open to interpretation, which makes it very personal. I began to examine the origins of the Seven Principles, and discovered that at the time of delivery, there had actually been quite a few more.

So, who *was* Robert Owen? I did more digging and found out. He was a Welsh textile manufacturer, who invested in and managed a large textile mill at New Lanark in Scotland (creating the New Lanark Village). He was also well known for his efforts to improve the conditions of the factory workers.

Further digging revealed that Mrs Britten, an English medium, received information from the Spirit World through her trance mediumship. Robert Owen (deceased) was one of her spirit inspirers, whose communications helped her compile the *Ten Spiritual Commandments* and the *Ten Laws of Right*; and so significant were they, that they were later modified and turned into the Seven Principles.

I read the *Commandments* and *Laws of Right* over and over again. They were difficult to understand for they were written in nineteenth-century English, so I had, first, to interpret them into modern English. Their content was intriguing. It seemed to stipulate that although Spiritualism is a religion, it is very dependent on science. We have 'God'; and we have the laws of nature and physics, all existing hand in hand, one necessarily entwined with the other.

When I read *The New Revelation* by Sir Arthur Conan Doyle and *The Rock of Truth*, by Arthur Findlay, these books seemed to confirm this fact. I went on to read *The Fall of the House of Sceptics: Science and Psychic Phenomena* and *Science and the Afterlife Experience: Evidence for the Immortality of Consciousness,* both by Chris Carter. I also read *Multiple Universes and Religion*, and *Spirit of the New Millennium: The Ultimate Theory*, each by Frank Newman.

Chris Carter and Frank Newman referred to the science behind Spiritualism. One interesting part, was the concept of Quantum Physics: the study of the atom and what it is made up of. I already had a vague idea that the world is made up of matter, and that matter, in turn, is made up of things called atoms, and all this is energy. I tried to read physics books, but the information was difficult to understand. I finally resorted to *Ducksters Education Site*, an online website for children, which proved very informative, and suited me just fine. But my research still failed to answer the fundamental question: what was going on with me?

3

THE SEVEN MODERN-DAY PRINCIPLES

To enhance my understanding, I decided it was time to review the Seven Modern-Day Principles. I searched the Website for the Spiritualists' National Union and found their interpretation.

The Fatherhood of God

By a study of nature, that is, by trying to understand the laws of cause and effect, which govern all that is happening around us, we recognise that there is a creative force in the universe. This force, or energy, not only created the whole universe but life itself in its many forms and is continuing to create today, creating, not from nothing, but of itself, and the effects of this eternal creation can be seen around us today, even in the farthest reaches of outer space, as has been shown in its astounding grandeur by the remarkable photographs taken through the medium of the Hubble telescope. This leads us to acknowledge that God, the Creative Force, manifests directly or indirectly in all things. We know this power as God and, as we are a part of the life created by God, we acknowledge God as our Father.

The Brotherhood of Man

Because we all come from the same universal Life source we are, in effect, one large family. This means that all mankind is part of a brotherhood. A brotherhood is a community for mutual support and comfort; we are all members of the same divine family. We have to understand the needs of other individuals in order to assist them as part of our service to each other. As we learn to give, so must we also learn to receive, thereby achieving the necessary balance for our lives.

The Communion of Spirits and the Ministry of Angels

Many Spiritualists consider this as the key Principle. All religions believe in life after death but only Spiritualism shows it is true by demonstrating that communication with departed spirits can, and does, take place. Spiritualist churches and centres provide many of the venues where communication, through Mediumship, is possible and many loved ones and friends take advantage of this opportunity to continue to show an interest in our welfare and us. There are spirit people who are dedicated to the welfare and service of humanity. Silver Birch (one of the many spirit guides) brought inspiration and teaching through the mediumship of Maurice Barbanell (one of Spiritualism's many pioneers). Others work in the healing ministry to bring support along the pathway of humanity.

The Continuous Existence of the Human Soul

Matter and energy cannot be created or destroyed. This is an old scientific axiom which research continues to confirm. If we accept this, and there is no reason why we should not, we need to know what happens when the present form of energy reaches the end of its viability. The answer is, simply, that it changes its manifestation. Spirit is energy and is therefore indestructible. On the death of the physical body the spirit continues as an integral part of a world which interpenetrates our world in different dimensions: this other world is referred to as the spirit world. In spirit life we have a spirit body that is a replica of our earthly body but it is a much finer form. We are the same individuals in every way, with the same personalities and characteristics, and we change only by progression, or otherwise, as a result of our own efforts.

Personal Responsibility

This Principle is the one which places responsibility for wrongful thoughts and deeds where it belongs, with the individual. It is the acceptance of responsibility for every aspect of our lives; and the use to which we put our lives depends entirely upon ourselves. It is not possible for any other person or outside influence to interfere with our spiritual development, unless we are willing to allow this. As we are given freedom of choice (freewill), so also are we given the ability to recognise what is right and wrong for our own spirituality. We are personally responsible for all our words, deeds and thoughts.

Compensation and Retribution Hereafter for all the Good and Evil Deeds done on Earth

As with all other Principles, natural laws apply; this one echoes the Law of Cause and Effect ('what goes around, comes around'). One cannot be cruel and vindictive towards others and expect love and popularity in return. It should be understood that the compensatory or retributive effects of this law operate now, on earth: they do not wait until we begin to live our lives in the spirit world. With this understanding we can try to put right wrongs that we know we have done before we pass from this life.

Eternal Progress Open to every Human Soul

In most humans there exists the desire for progress and to every human soul belongs the power to advance in wisdom and love. All who desire to tread the path that leads to spiritual wisdom and understanding are able to do so. The rate of progress is directly proportional to the desire for mental and spiritual understanding. It is the realisation that our soul is a part of eternity and the road to progress is open any time we choose to walk it. This can help us come to terms with the challenges of this world.

So, what did all of this mean? Well, for a start, I didn't believe for a minute that those in the Spirit World were sitting on their haunches, doing nothing. No. They were out there doing things. They were interacting with us, humans, trying to give *us* inspiration to make *us* decide how to render our world a better place. And for *that* to happen, they clearly knew how to work with the laws of nature: maybe even tweak them a bit. And for *that* to be, at least some of them had to have a better understanding of science than we, in the physical world, did.

The job ahead was going to be hard. I wasn't a scientist, but something was driving me on. I knew I had some kind of task to complete, which meant I *had* to understand: up to a point, anyway. If I didn't, I might spend the rest of my life thinking that not only was I psychotic, so too were my three mobile phones. So, if not to prove my own sanity, I had, at the very least, to uphold the reputations of my phones. I needed to speak to Dad again.

4

THE SCIENCE OF LIFE AND GOD

The Committee of the Glasgow Association of Spiritualists invited me to join them in September 2017. I began to chair many of the services and meet a variety of visiting mediums. I'd already met Jacqui, and having discussed my photographs with her, now decided to explain to her what I was trying to achieve. She understood and agreed to help.

On 2 October 2017, I started the first of six interviews that took a couple of years to complete, in the hope of finding enough answers to broaden my knowledge of this deep and very complex subject. My intention was to try and obtain a better idea of how things came to be, and where we, as human beings, fit in.

C: I've heard so many different theories about the 'Creation' and where we fit into it as a human being, and it gets very confusing. I've concluded from a lot of the modern stuff I've read, that we're living here on earth, in a world of electromagnetic energy fields that all react with one another.

J: Yes.

C: What would my father say about that?

J: He agrees in the sense that we're all slightly different levels of frequency. Does that make sense?

C: Yes, thank you. I also believe that we, as human beings, are made up of matter, and we're made of dense matter to suit the frequency of earth's energy fields. Would my father agree?

J: Yes.

C: Now, matter, again ourselves, is made up of atoms.

J: Yes.

C: And if we go further still, atoms can be subdivided into particles; and these particles are: protons, neutrons, electrons, plus a number of other things, which I'll not go into. And this is the basis of Quantum Physics.

J: Yes.

C: One thing I would like to know: *is* the Spirit World composed of finer forms of matter?

J: Yes.

C: So, the atoms making up their matter must be of a finer kind?

J: Yes. They're not as thick as ours. Our human bodies are thicker matter. The only way I can put it: it's like jelly. You can put your hand into jelly, but you'll feel it. If you put your hand into mist, you can't. Does that make sense?

C: Yes.

J: Denser. We're denser than spirit. Spirits are like mist.

C: So, we're jelly and they're mist!

J: Yes.

C: Now the next important thing I want to consider is that matter (which is us), is energy. So, we are energy.

J: Yes.

C: Energy (which is us) cannot be created or destroyed, it can only change from one form to another. Would my dad agree with that?

J: Yes.

C: It's probably not as simple as that.

J: No. But he does agree. Your dad's mind is different, though. Although he understands a lot of this, he has his own opinion, and always did have.

C: So, if I give an example. X-rays can be converted into matter by slowing down their rays.

J: I just heard: 'yes'.

C: And wood can be converted into heat energy by burning.

J: Yes.

C: That's the simple one.

J: Yes.

C: So, since energy cannot be destroyed, we (who are energy): we cannot be destroyed.

J: Yes.

C: As simple as that.

J: Yes.

C: The next thing I want to look at is my understanding of 'God', and where we fit in as individuals. My understanding of 'God' is that it's an energy source and a mass mind. So, this mass mind is energy. Do you agree with that?

J: Yes, but a mass mind of whom?

C: Is that what he's asked?

J: Who do *you* think 'God' is?

C: I was going to ask *him* the same question.

J: Your dad has just said that to me. He said: 'Who do *you* think 'God' is?' And I think he's saying that because, again, we have this 'God' picture where we assume it's one person. I don't think your dad ever did. I don't think your dad ever had that belief that 'God' was one person. Your dad had a different kind of belief. I'm not saying he wasn't a Christian, or anything, because I think he was brought up within that, but for him, he sees energy in a different kind of variable state.

C: My understanding of 'God' is energy, I have to say. Is that my dad's understanding?

J: Yes.

C: Is that the understanding he had when he was here?

J: Yes. But your dad never realised the depth of it until he went to Spirit. And I think there's lots of variables in there, because it won't always be the same energies. It will rotate. So, 'God' will move like we do.

5

THE PHYSICAL AND THE SPIRITUAL

So, all very interesting. Energy is constantly changing and moving. Nothing remains the same. Energy always develops. As my research progressed, my understanding of the books I'd read by Chris Carter and Frank Newman deepened, and the SNU's *Philosophy of Spiritualism* threw more light on the meaning of the Seven Principles. Finally, betwixt and between, I was able to determine the following facts.

Our physical and spirit bodies

Not only do we have a physical body, we have a spirit one too: and in fact, our spirit came into being long before our physical body. Furthermore, there is a huge distinction between the physical brain and Mind, and this is fundamental to understanding the philosophy behind Spiritualism.

The brain

The brain is matter. It is made of physical cells, which in turn are made of atoms that are broken down into particles. The main particles are protons, electrons and neutrons; and it's the electrons that cause each atom to vibrate at a particular frequency: in our case, our denser physical human frequency. So, despite all appearances, our brain is far from still. It vibrates away. And because the rest of our body is made of physical cells, with their own particles, that means the rest of our physical body is also vibrating away.

The role of the brain

The brain is there to coordinate the smooth running of the physical body. Our nervous system is attached to our brain. Electrical impulses run through this system, and its connection with the brain allows our physical body to work properly. The brain processes data using our five physical senses: touch, sight, hearing, smell and taste.

The fate of the brain

Because the brain is made of physical matter, once our physical body dies, so does the brain. The brain is no different from our other physical organs: the liver and heart, for instance. The brain decays like the body and returns to nature.

The Mind

Mind is consciousness and memory. It stores our thoughts, feelings, emotions and memories and has no predisposition to colour, creed or sex. Mind is energy, but not a consistent energy. It moves and changes, developing as we learn. Mind and Spirit are inseparable, and for the purpose of simplicity I have decided to consider them as being one and the same.

Mind and Spirit

Mind is the clever part of Spirit. It drives the brain. It has no permanent shape, and can fit nicely around every part of our physical body when it blends. Just as the brain connects with the nervous system, so does Mind, and that's why we feel emotion in different parts of our body. Unfortunately, the natural function of Mind becomes constrained by our physical beliefs, fears and compunctions. We start to talk about the 'human mind', and it is the 'human mind' that restricts us in what we do.

Interpenetration of atoms on different frequencies

Since spirit atoms are much finer than physical atoms, they vibrate on a higher frequency; because Spirit operates on this different frequency, the Spirit World is believed to interpenetrate the physical world (a bit like different radio frequencies crossing each other), only most of us are not spiritually aware enough to perceive this.

The origin of Spirit

Our individual spirits come from one energy source: the Mass Mind. Our understanding of what the Mass Mind is, is very subjective. Whether we consider it to be 'God', or 'Universal Energy', either way, it is made up of particles. Whatever you call it, its energy complies with the First Law of Thermodynamics: it cannot be created or destroyed, it can only change form.

How we are formed from the Mass Mind

In order to understand how our spirit is individualised, we have to look at the particles of the Mass Mind. During the interviews, I'd managed to go as far back as I could to the beginning of things, but discovered that even the Spirit World doesn't know everything. Dad was able to go as far back as a collision of particles, followed by the creation of *an intelligent entity*, as a consequence of which, there resulted other *intelligent entities*, known as Spirit.

Each particle is a tiny, tiny seed of Spirit: a spirit seed. Each seed is magnetised, so is able to send out signals indicating what it needs. As the signal goes out, other tiny particles, or, spirit seeds, are attracted or repelled. The ones that are attracted start coming in and attaching themselves. Molecules are formed. These molecules then bond with other molecules until separate entities are formed, and these mature and eventually become an individual spirit with enough intellect to blend with a human body.

How our spirit blends with our physical human body

To begin with, the spirit energy must be adequately evolved to be able to blend with a human baby. The energy that blends with the likes of a cat or dog is less evolved, and not suitable. Energy must be like for like. The intelligence of a spirit form is quite specific, and the process has to be viable. At the time of physical conception, chemical and electrical reactions take place and there is an energy connection. This means that as the physical embryo is nurtured inside its mother, energy is able to flow back and forth between the embryo and the spirit energy. The spirit energy (which remains connected to the Spirit World) will always function on its higher vibration. Memories develop and channels are formed, but birth puts a stop to this easy back and forth process. It is then down to us, as physical beings, to decide how far we wish to restore the connection in order to develop our own particular spirituality. Mediums have developed their awareness and are able to attune and connect with the Spirit World.

How the brain and Mind work together

The brain and Mind work hand in hand, but their roles are quite different. If we cut ourselves, the brain kicks in and starts giving instructions on how to repair the damaged area; but the Mind is a much deeper thing. It asks questions: How did I do that? Why did I do that? What have I learned from doing that?

The fate of the spirit body when our physical body dies

We've already looked at the scientific rule that energy cannot be created or destroyed, and this also applies to our individualised spirit energies: in other words, our consciousness. When our physical body dies (and its parts return to nature), our spirit body, continues to play an integral part within the universal energy by returning to the Spirit World.

6

DAD'S ROLE IN THE SPIRIT WORLD

I felt I was getting somewhere, but as the interviews progressed, I wanted to know more about Dad's role in the Spirit World. I soon discovered he was a healer, but not only that, he was an educator: an educator of young spirits as eager to learn in the Spirit World as we are in the physical world. It was on that note that I dared to ask him about angels.

C: Now, one thing I'd like to talk about, and it's something I've never really understood, is angels and the angelic realms. What's my dad's reaction to mentioning angelic realms?

J: He rolled his eyes at that.

C: Did he?

J: He doesn't see them like that. He sees them as helpers.

C: OK. I'll tell you what my understanding has been. I've been led to believe that they are highly evolved souls (spirits) that are there to help souls like ourselves.

J: Yes.

C: So, Jesus is a helper in the Spirit World?

J: Jesus is a healer.

C: OK. But these helpers, as opposed to angels, do they exist in the Spirit World?

J: Yes. But they're a level unto themselves.

C: And has my father had contact with them in any way?

J: The healers.

C: So, has he had contact with Jesus?

J: The healers, yes. But I think again, our perception of Jesus is not what your dad's is.

C: OK.

J: It's different.

C: So, we're really looking at them as highly evolved helpers, some of whom are healers. I assume they do *not* have wings?

J: Flies have wings.

C: Is that what he said?

J: Yes: flies have wings. Your dad could be quite cynical about things.

C: You better believe it.

J: But your dad does understand why people would want to believe in angels.

C: And why is that?

J: Because it gives them comfort. But he said a lot of that isn't real.

Your dad has to be logical.

C: So, when people talk about our guardian angels, what do they mean?

J: They are just other energies that are helping us on our path.

C: So, how do our helpers help us? Is it with our thoughts?

J: With our thoughts. They just help guide us. They maybe give us a dream, or, an understanding of something. They can make you feel emotion. It's just how they touch your energy.

C: And it affects the way you feel. You react to it, basically?

J: Yes.

C: I'm wondering if my dad is aware of the works of Emmanuel Swedenborg (*Eighteenth-Century Swedish theologian, scientist, philosopher and mystic, best known for his book on the Afterlife: Heaven and Hell*), who said he conversed with angels for over twenty years. Is he aware of the works?

J: Yes.

C: What's his opinion of the work?

J: Your dad says he would have called him a madman. But I think he would have done that in his life (physical). He would have said: 'He's a madman! You can't speak to angels!' But your dad understands it in a different sense now, and not necessarily with the angel connotation.

C: Would it have been with higher evolved spirits he (*Swedenborg*) was conversing?

J: Again, it's this human thing that we have of having to put a picture to something to acknowledge what it is. I think, yes, he did converse with what he perceived to be angels, but they not necessarily were. Beings of light. Your dad doesn't perceive him (*Swedenborg*) like that now, but he would have done.

7

GEORGE AND DYSENTERY

I was continuing to put a picture together, and as the parameters widened, I realised that dad's input was not restricted to matters discussed during our personal encounters, but to comments he had made in the past to other mediums, who were demonstrating on the Church platform.

J: Your dad's got a hat on now. He's just put a hat on. I'm finding him funny. He's just being funny. It's like a cap. Who's George?

C: Ask him! I keep getting George through. I was told he might be someone he (Dad) was at university with. Is that correct?

J: I think it might be, but he wore a cap. George wore a cap. You might have a picture of him.

C: I'll go through the stuff.

J: It's definitely George. He's got a flat cap on. But your dad's making a joke with him.

C: My dad said he (Dad) was very dour when he studied. Is there a reason he keeps bringing George through? Is it to make me lighten up a bit?

J: I think it's to make your dad lighten up. Because your dad became very serious. Towards the end I think the Parkinson's made him deadly serious. (*I'd already made Jacqui aware that Dad had suffered from Parkinson's disease.*)

C: Yes.

J: And changed his attitude. Did your dad have dysentery?

C: In India he did, on and off.

J: I don't know whether dysentery affected him later in his life, and it wasn't until later, he realised that that was part of what happened.

C: Would dysentery have had an effect on the Parkinson's?

J: I think so.

C: How funny. When my dad's mind wasn't right, David once said: 'Your father keeps talking about a situation in India that caused him to get Parkinson's.'

J: It was dysentery.

C: Is that what he was trying to say to David?

J: I think so. And I think your dad, *he* was still there, but his human mind wasn't always. But *he* was still there. He's adamant about that. I think it was the dysentery, and do you know why? Because my dad had it, and my dad said that's how he lost his teeth. It was because of the dysentery: so, I keep seeing teeth.

C: So, that's your correlation there. That's interesting.

J: Very.

C: Because it's mentioned in the letters. Dysentery, bowel diseases and things like that. He was always catching something off the patients. The conditions weren't great, so, the doctor would end up in bed!

8

BACTERIA

Things were moving at a steady pace. I'd covered a bit of science: enough for my non-scientific mind, anyway. But now I wanted to look more closely at the Principles of Spiritualism. The original Principles, given to Mrs Britten, had specified quite clearly that science and the laws of nature played a predominant part, so, on the afternoon of Wednesday, 29 August 2018, my questions under my arm, I trundled back to Jacqui's for a spot of elucidation.

If I'd thought I was in charge of the interview, then I was wrong. Dad had his own agenda. As I rattled through the *Ten Spiritual Commandments* and the *Creed of the Spirits* (all written in nineteenth-century English, of course), Dad quickly changed the subject.

J: Bacteria.

C: What? Bacteria?

J: There's something about bacteria. I'm trying to understand what I'm getting. The process of elimination and bacteria.

C: Is he jumping forward to Darwin's Theory? (*Darwin's Theory of Evolution was something I'd studied whilst compiling questions: unbeknown to Jacqui.*)

J: I think so. I think he wants to talk about the way organisms change and alter, and how you adapt to the place that you're in. Things change, and Spirit is similar in that sense.

C: This does cover some of the questions I've prepared for later on. Is he wanting me to jump forward and discuss that today?

J: Just go to that bit.

C: If I can find it.

J: I didn't know what I was saying there.

C: It's Darwinism. Whilst I'm looking for it, can you ask him if he has anything he wants to tell me?

J: Bacteria! I don't know whether your dad looked into bacteria and how different types of bacteria affect the body; and how there's good bacteria that's needed to counteract the bad bacteria; and how they work in conjunction with each other. It kind of creates an infinity of work, and your dad talks about that applying to Spirit also. How you have to have a life to have a death, and have to use your spirit and understand it. They work together. So, the Darwinian approach: that is all about how things change and build and alter, and how the atoms change, depending on where you are. Whether you need fins for water, or legs for land. And it's the same with spirits.

C: I've found my questions. And that was something I was going to ask: does it also apply to Spirit?

J: The two.

C: Darwin's *Theory of Evolution* shows how humans and animals share a common ancestry. We started out as apes, but we've evolved into humans. Is that right?

J: Yes.

C: If we go back to the beginning, we discussed the collision of particles, which was followed by the creation of *an intelligent entity*, as a consequence of which, there resulted other *intelligent entities*, known as Spirit. The question I'd like to ask is: in view of the *Theory of Evolution*, did Spirit, destined to incarnate into humans (like my spirit, which was *destined* at the time to finally incarnate into me), did my spirit at that time start with the apes? Or, was it different kinds of spirit?

J: Not evolved. Not evolved spirit.

C: Not evolved?

J: Yes. If you see the structure of a human or animal, it's the same. It's like a machine, and the energy that is attracted into the machine is what creates the person.

C: So, it's a more advanced energy that is attracted to the machinery of the human body?

J: You need a more advanced energy for it to control and work with that brain.

C: So, humans obviously evolved over time, and their brains improved?

J: Yes.

C: So, *my* spirit that was ready to go into *my* body (physical): where was it in the Spirit World at the time of the apes and no humans?

J: It would have been part of the universal energy, where all the energies come together.

C: So, it wouldn't yet have been evolved enough to go into a human?

J: Maybe not quite ready then. Maybe going through the understanding process.

C: That makes sense. So, Darwin concludes that all species on earth, including humans, evolved over time through the process of Natural Selection.

J: Bacteria!

C: Bacteria! And Natural Selection is survival of the fittest.

J: Bacteria!

C: And adaptation to the environment.

J: Bacteria!

C: What part did Spirit have in this?

J: I don't know whether they did. I don't know whether they were just around, or part of the energy and had to let things create themselves. Does that make sense?

C: Yes, it does.

J: And that mixes with my own brain. Although your dad is saying this, and I'm allowing it, I would have liked to think that Spirit had a hand in it, but I think he's right.

C: When we have a physical body, it comes alive when Spirit comes?

J: We're a machine. If Spirit steps out, what's left?

C: Just a dead machine.

J: Yes. We're a car. Spirit has the key. They drive us.

C: Is that what he said?

J: Yes. They (Spirit) drive us. But we (humans) will it. Once they've activated the brain (human), we then have human will. And I think that's different to Spirit, because you have a will to achieve and do different things, and reach a certain level.

C: So, going back to bacteria (good bacteria and bad bacteria) it's the right bacteria that is letting the physical live. Is that right?

J: Yes. I think some of your dad's work, some of the work he did in the past, will come out. Come to fruition, more in the future, where he looked at bacteria and different things. How to fix different diseases. I don't know what he did, but I think he wrote something on how certain bacteria won't die. I don't know what that was, or how he wrote it, and I don't know whether that's to do with when he was ill. Once you have bacteria in your body, sometimes they never go. They might lie dormant. But that (new research) might be coming to fruition, soon, I think. Someone will publish something, and it will be very similar to your dad's ideas.

C: I do actually have 'bacteria' mentioned somewhere in my questions.

J: I've never mentioned bacteria before, until today. And it just came in, like: boom! So, there's something about bacteria and Spirit and how they are linked. There's something about them being energy-linked. I think what happens is, it may be that energy will kick start bacteria, without knowing. I think there's something about the energy (from our spirit) getting the bacteria (pause): it's like putting something electric into us. It's like giving it electricity to feed it.

C: Like a plug? An electric current?

J: Yes.

We then changed the subject and had a lengthy discussion about mountains, volcanos and the composition of the earth and its magnetic fields. In an earlier interview Dad had mentioned plate tectonics, and for some reason I felt drawn to reintroduce the topic. I soon discovered why.

C: We talked about plate tectonics. I looked it up. Big lumps of land made of a combination of the crust and outer mantle (of the earth). Also called the lithosphere. And they move very slowly, about a couple of inches a year. That's the movement of mountains and things, isn't it? You find them either on land, or under the sea.

J: The Giant's Causeway runs from Scotland to Ireland, and it's the same. But you can't see 90% of it. It runs under the sea (Irish Sea) from Scotland to Ireland.

C: Has he just said that?

J: Yes.

C: That's interesting.

J: So, you might not see 90% of what you think you're looking at. You only ever see the tip of the iceberg, and it's the same when you talk about Spirit. You'll maybe only have a connection to 1% of Spirit.

C: Just a very small proportion.

J: Yes. Because you're shielded. They shield you from what you don't need.

C: How do they know what you do and don't need?

J: They're aware of what you're doing. They're aware of your capabilities to deal with spirit energy and how much you can deal with. Some people usurp energy and connect to 2%, and even up to 10%.

C: That's quite a lot, isn't it?

J: Yes. But then you need to look at what's going on with that person. Are they having breakdowns? Are they *not* dealing with the bigger level of energy? Can they cope with it? It might cause problems with their clarity. Clearness of thought. Principles are personal perceptions. You live by your own commandments. Do not relent to others' processes.

C: Don't relax your own principles to conform to others.

J: Yes.

And then it dawned on me. The original Principles! We'd just gone right back to what I'd tried to discuss in the first place: before Dad had quite bluntly introduced the topic of bacteria. I flicked through my paperwork and found the information I needed. I started to read it out, but he stopped me at 'Almsgiving'.

C: Almsgiving: that's very old-fashioned, but help the sick and the poor.

J: Sometimes the sick and the poor are yourself. Look after yourself.

C: We should not fear physical death for there is no eternal punishment, only eternal progress.

J: When somebody dies, why do we say, 'rest in peace', when they're *not* dead?

C: They're *not* dead, are they?

J: And even other religions that believe in an afterlife, they still say: 'rest in peace'. And I don't think you'd rest in peace. Once your engine's done and your motor's finished, your soul (spirit) doesn't rest. Your soul progresses, and I think you move on further than you ever would in this life. I think *this* is more 'rest in peace', compared to what's going to happen when you go over.

C: You're going to work when you go over.

J: Yes. And I think 'rest in peace' is wrong.

C: You're right.

J: I'm going to write: 'do *not* rest in peace, my friend'!

C: So, we should not fear physical death, for there is *no* eternal punishment, only eternal progress.

J: Yes.

C: Which is basically...

J: What we just spoke about. Yes. Exactly what we just said.

C: There is no devil.

J: Only in the details.

C: When our spirit returns to the Spirit World, we judge ourselves and look at all the good and bad things we did during our existence in the physical world. Is that right?

J: Yes.

C: There is no atonement for sin: we have no option other than to try and progress.

J: Yes. Was your dad deaf in one ear?

C: What? Yes.

J: Left ear?

C: Can't remember. I'll ask my mum.

J: It's this one (*points to left*): it keeps going dull.

C: He was definitely deaf.

J: Did he have big ears?

C: (*laughing*) I think he had quite big ears.

J: Not 'sticky-out' ones.

C: No.

J: But they were quite large. He's laughing. I'm finding him funny. His head's cold.

C: What?

J: He said: *'My head's cold'*! Was he losing his hair?

C: He was balding up the top.

J: That's maybe why he says his head's cold.

C: Tell him to put a hat on!

J: I did. He just laughed when I said that.

It was becoming clear that those in the Spirit World certainly don't lose their sense of humour when they pass over. George (whoever he was) and his flat cap. Dad's cold head and big ears. But caps, bald heads and big ears weren't going to help me with my investigation: or, were they?

C: We're supposed to be discussing the Principles! Spiritualism will only accept theories about the Spirit World if they have been proven and corroborated.

J: Evidence-based!

C: Any physical phenomena, witnessed by us, must be passed as indisputable evidence, and supported by the science that lies within the laws of nature and physics.

J: Got to be backed up! Got to be backed up!

C: It must open the way to new scientific research.

J: There needs to be new scientific research.

C: According to the Principles, 'God' and 'Science' are necessarily entwined; and the final bit here: we must do the best we can, and try to be good.

J: I think that's just a normal human function, isn't it? We try to be good because that's what our parents tell us to do.

C: When we return to the Spirit World, we will be reunited with our discarnate loved ones; we will also review our lives as we lived them in the physical world and understand that it is up to each of us (our personal responsibility) to take steps to develop and progress our spirit. We can be guided, but no one can act on our behalf.

J: Yes. I agree with that. But I don't think you'll meet *all* your loved ones.

C: Not *all* of them?

J: Well, would you want to be with them *all* here? Would you want to be with everybody here?

C: Probably not.

J: I think we pick and choose. I think we see the people we want to see. It'll be like this. You dip in and out.

C: Is that what my father says? You can choose?

J: Yes.

C: Can I ask him, since we've been discussing Mrs Britten's work, has he ever met her?

J: No.

C: And what does he think of her Principles?

J: He says they're OK. But I think it's the interpretation. You have to look at who's interpreting them. That's why you have to have your own interpretation of them. It's like the *Ten Commandments*. You can say: 'Thou shalt not steal.' We're taught this.

C: But what happens in different circumstances?

J: This is it. If you have no food, and you have four children to feed, you have to steal to feed them. So, I think there's a balance there. And I think your dad understands that there's more of a balance there than just what they say as rules.

C: Did Emma Hardinge Britten *really* receive information from the Spirit World during trance mediumship? Primarily from Robert Owen? Can you ask my dad?

J: I think, 'partly' comes in. Yes.

C: Does he know who the other communicators were?

J: No. He keeps saying: 'her own gains'.

C: Her own gains?

J: Yes. I don't know whether he thinks Emma Hardinge Britten was gaining, herself. I don't think he rates her. I think he's trying to see it as: how can you provide evidence of who spoke to her, unless there is physical evidence to prove it? And if you can't, then your dad doesn't want to really know. Your Dad likes the evidence. You know, like a court case. You would have to prove who murdered who.

C: Corroboration.

J: Yes. And your dad likes that. And I feel if you go back to his notes (*letters he wrote in India*), there's evidence throughout them about how things changed, and if things altered. Go back to the mosquitos and how they infect. Do you understand? It's that kind of thing. I think you need to look at what's important and clarify it. Because what I'm getting from your dad is that it's pointless asking the same question in three different ways. Does that make sense?

C: Yes.

J: He wants you to look at it logically.

C: Concentrate on the medical side of things?

J: I think he wanted to go over things. The feeling I get from your dad today is that because he started off really quickly (I was surprised at the bacteria stuff), he's clearly been thinking about how to orient you.

C: Orientate me?

J: Yes. And how to deal with the processes that you have. So, I think he's trying to organise you. And that's a good thing! I think he's setting you up for having everything right.

9

TRYING TO GET IT RIGHT

So that was that. I would have to go back over the letters at some point to search for facts and see where they would lead me. During the interviews, Dad had given out a lot of very personal information: stuff that provided great corroboration, but didn't appear to be relevant to this project. There were also the odd crazy comments, like:

'Your dad likes cheese,' and *'your dad likes chocolate.'*

He did, indeed. But at the time, I'd discounted these observations, until on reflection, I realised that maybe the comments actually mattered. I was beginning to follow Dad's train of thought. If he mentioned *'cheese'* he probably meant penicillin; whereas, if he referred to *'chocolate'*, he no doubt wanted to explain the 'ins and outs' of antioxidants. My mind was boggling.

Then remembering the comment about Dad's 'big ears' and 'cold head', I uncovered a photograph: and was able to confirm that 'big ears' did, indeed, form part of the equation. As for his hair, although it was thinning on the top, the photo could neither prove, nor disprove baldness. But as I continued to study the picture, I noticed something else. I observed a scar on the left side of his neck: something I'd totally forgotten about. I asked my mum to remind me, and she clarified that it was to do with tuberculosis, which he'd had as a baby, caught from one of the labourers on his father's dairy farm: *mycobacterium tuberculosis*.

So, we'd gone back to bacteria. Here was another type of bacterial infection attacking Dad, this time as a young child. Had this also (like dysentery) contributed towards the onset of Parkinson's disease?

Dad was making me work hard. He seemed to be further widening the parameters of study. My head was buzzing, just like one of those dastardly little mosquitoes. I needed a fix (not a blood fix, of course), but a knowledge fix.

10

BACTERIA AND THE IMMUNE SYSTEM

I'd already established that Dad wanted me to look for evidence. He'd indicated that he'd written something on how certain bacteria won't die, and that new research might be coming out relating to that. As I pondered over this, I realised there was also a hint of something else. I was thinking of an earlier interview, during which, I'd reeled off the *Ten Spiritual Commandments* and the *Creed of the Spirits*. Dad had stopped me at the 'devil'.

C: *There is no devil.*

J: *Only in the details.*

Only in the details? What did that mean? Was there something else? Something more important that was still outstanding? Something I should have identified? Had I already glossed over it? What was this mysterious element? There was only one way to find out: go back and look at what we'd already discussed, then progress further.

I'd found Dad's reference to there being a connection between dysentery and Parkinson's disease fascinating, so decided to research the matter, and was pleasantly surprised to find something of interest. I also made a list of the main diseases that Dad had dealt with in India. My intention was to 'pick his brain': or, rather, his

Mind. I put my questions together and prepared myself for another interview. I wasn't surprised when Dad prompted Jacqui to re-introduce what was fast becoming his favourite subject: bacteria.

C: I'm going to ask about dysentery and Parkinson's. We worked out during the last interview that there might be an association. 'Teeth' came to you, Jacqui, with your own father.

J: He lost his teeth.

C: So, I looked this up. I'll read the following article:

'A genetic link has been discovered between the immune system and Parkinson's disease. Scientists have discovered new evidence that Parkinson's disease may have an infectious or autoimmune origin. This is with the University of Washington: 2010. Researchers at that time detected a new association with the HLA (human leukocyte antigen) region, which contains a large number of genes related to the immune system function in humans. They're having a fresh look at the possible role of infections, inflammation and autoimmunity in Parkinson's disease.'

J: Where's your immune system?

C: I don't know. Is this what he's asking?

J: No. *I'm* asking you.

C: Don't know.

J: It's nowhere because it's all over. It's bacteria. Your immune system is bacteria.

C: So, the good bacteria?

J: That fights the bad bacteria. Sometimes it overtakes it; and if it can feel like it's fighting against certain parts of the body in certain ways, and if it affects the nervous system in some ways, that's where I feel that Parkinson's is involved. It affects certain things, but it's bacteria. I think you need to round everything up together, like Parkinson's, dysentery, all bacteria and dementia.

C: And dementia?

J: I think Parkinson's is connected to dementia.

C: He (Dad) was in and out of it (dementia); but it's been because of the Parkinson's?

J: I think it's because of the nerves. The nerves stopped working: the ones that were supplying areas of the brain. I think it's all bacteria. I think you need to look at bacteria: gut bacteria. Gut. It's the gut. The gut is the immune system. And do you know, I'm wondering why your dad's coming up with this. I've recently had lots of thoughts about how important your gut is to being well. And I think your dad might be right.

C: I've looked into respiratory infections he dealt with in India. Does he want to discuss that?

J: I think they are secondary to the bacteria. I think it's the bacteria that starts the infection off, and it depends where it goes in the body, or where the bacteria settle.

C: There are also bowel infections.

J: The same. Gut. That comes through the gut.

C: And liver abscesses?

J: Liver abscesses are quite funny. I think they come through the blood being faulty, or, there are issues with the blood.

C: And anaemia?

J: The gut not absorbing the minerals. Absorption of the Bs? The Bs?

Ah! Absorption of the B vitamins.

C: And tetanus?

J: Different again.

C: But the main thing, I feel, is that Dad wants to discuss malaria and bacteria.

J: The bacteria and the malaria go hand in hand: and it can be quicker with some people, and harsher, where the disease can take hold very quickly; and in others, bacteria levels are so good in their body that it doesn't necessarily cause them that much harm.

C: And does that have anything to do with why the mosquito is more inclined to bite some people more than others?

J: I think the mosquitoes bite everybody, but it's who reacts. And it's to do with their levels of good bacteria compared to the bad. And it also depends on how strong they've become: like their immune system, as such.

C: If the immune system is weakened?

J: Yes.

C: So, if we go back to dysentery, and if you have a predisposition to Parkinson's disease.

J: And he did.

C: And then you get a bacterial infection like dysentery, you're likely to develop Parkinson's disease?

J: Not *likely*. The percentage is different with everybody. And it's to do with how your body deals with the bacteria.

C: Bacteria again. And obviously, with his body, the immune system wasn't up to dealing with it.

J: Yes.

C: So, it's been bacterial infections like dysentery?

J: But I think it was even after that. It was the different types of infections he had over the years. I don't know whether he had a liver infection, or, a liver/kidney issue?

C: He had to have liver biopsies because he was on Methotrexate for severe psoriasis. It might have something to do with that.

J: There's something about that.

C: Methotrexate?

J: No. The liver. I don't know if there was a build-up there of bacteria.

C: He had a lot of urinary infections.

J: Yes. And I think it was maybe just a build-up in the system. And while the body is fighting one area, then it can't work on others; and others fail. It's balancing the machine.

C: We're still with this machine, aren't we?

J: Yes. But I keep seeing the old-fashioned scales that look like that: they balance at the top and you have a plate.

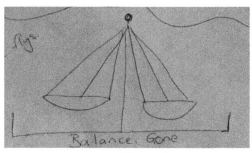

C: You'd have that for measuring out medicines: the chemist had that.

J: Yes.

C: But he's referring to the balance of the human body, isn't he? The physical body?

J: Yes, I think so. There's something about getting the balance right, because the balance wasn't right. Balance. Balance gone. Did his balance totally go?

C: Yes. He had no balance with the Parkinson's.

J: Gone.

C: He had no balance.

J: Balance gone. Did he start falling over on one side, first?

C: I can't remember if it was particularly one side, but he was very bad on his feet. Would my dad say that it was because he was in India he would get more infections later on? And that that aggravated the gene for Parkinson's?

J: I just think the different types of bacteria, and not necessarily in India. But it's because the bacteria couldn't die. And you need a certain amount of redress with the temperature to bring the bacteria under control, and that didn't happen in India. But I don't think it started there. I don't think it started in India. I think it was already in his body.

C: Would that have anything to do with his mastoid? He had Mastoiditis, and had to have surgery.

J: I've got to say it goes back to being young. I think there was a predisposition for him, because of his family genetics. And actually, I know it (Parkinson's disease) came on his mum's side; but I think it was connected to his mum's grandparents; or, the grandfather in particular. So, his great-grandfather would have been predisposed to it also. So, I think it's been genetics through the family. So, it's in his system and how the bacteria react with it. Does that make sense?

C: Yes.

11

DAD'S PAST

So that was that. Dad had given me an abundance of information. He'd even alluded to the TB infection he'd had when a baby.

J: I've got to say it (bacterial infections) goes back to being young.

But I still wasn't satisfied. I felt I was chasing my tail. I hadn't as yet managed to identify the specific research Dad seemed to be referring to: only the fact that his ideas from the 1950s, would appear in the not-too-distant future in the form of new research. Unsure what to do next, I decided to delve into his past.

Dad was born on Overton Farm, Alexandria, Dunbartonshire (Scotland), on 13 March 1924. He was the youngest son of a dairy farmer. During his childhood and youth, he spent his time working hard at school, as well as milking the cows and selling the milk.

In 1941, at the age of seventeen, Dad became a medical student at Glasgow University, but in 1945, whilst still a student, he was forced to review medicine from a patient's perspective, when his mastoid was surgically removed, following an infection (Mastoiditis: another bacterial infection). He was admitted to the Ears, Nose and Throat Hospital, St Vincent's Street, Glasgow, where he was introduced to Mum (Reita): the nurse, assigned to look after him.

Dad qualified in 1946, and in 1947 became a resident at the Glasgow Royal Infirmary (middle row, far right).

In 1948, Mum and Dad got married, and moved to Falkirk, where Dad became an assistant general practitioner in a medical practice.

In 1951, after three years as an assistant, Dad saw an overseas post, advertised by the Tea Company, Williamson Magor, in the BMJ (British Medical Journal). They were looking for a principal medical officer, who would be responsible for the welfare of the labour forces (and families) on twelve tea estates, spread out against the Himalayan foothills, north of the Brahmaputra River in the Assam Valley, North East India.

Each tea garden had its own rudimentary hospital to treat the workers, who were expected to pluck the tea leaves, and produce the tea in the factory. Dad got the job, and in October 1951, he and Mum sailed to India. It was at this time that Dad began to write a series of letters to his parents in Scotland. When he died in 2004 Mum gave me his letters. I read them and quickly realised just how valuable they were, not only from a medical perspective, but from a geographic, economic and social one.

But more importantly, Dad had indicated, way back, that somewhere in these letters was a connection to the things that had been manifesting in my bedroom; and this connection was integral to my investigation. What I needed to do now, was find the evidence.

12

DAD'S LETTERS

Almost at Gibraltar, 19 October 1951

We went to the Coliseum (London Theatre) and saw a rather uninspiring "show" and were rather pleased that we could only get 4/- tickets in the "gods". We spent the night at a hotel near Victoria Station (London) so that we could make a quick get-away in the morning. When we arrived at the docks (Southampton) we spent hours in Customs but none of our baggage was opened. They do not appear to be very fussy about people leaving the country. When we boarded the ship (*the Batory*) and found our cabin, it was about 3 pm, and since we had not eaten, we were starving.

The meals on board are lovely. Every sitting has meat, and one can eat as much as one wishes. To begin with, the heaving of the boat upset us slightly, but we have got used to it. No one was sick, but quite a few passengers spent Wednesday in bed.

Near Port Said, 23 October 1951

We have been enjoying our trip along the Mediterranean very much indeed, and have dispensed with superfluous clothing.

(Dad: middle, Mum: far right)

I do not think we will have any bother at the Canal (Suez Canal) despite the News. The system of getting News on the ship is very poor. We do not get the BBC bulletins, and we have to rely on a daily type-written sheet that is pinned on the notice board.

Our evenings on the ship (*Mum and Dad: middle*) are filled with either films or dancing.

Tonight, we have the film: *Grounds for Marriage*. The films, in the main, have been quite enjoyable. Unfortunately, we lost an hour's sleep last night owing to the time change, and would have lost yet another hour had it not been for the change from British Summer Time to GMT at home.

When we arrived at Gibraltar, the few passengers who were disembarking and embarking, were taken in a small boat and we were not allowed to go ashore. The number of passengers and goods did not warrant a delay. The local boys from the nearby Spanish town, were soon out in their small boats, selling their wares. It was quite amusing watching them throw a line up to the deck, and passing stuff up in a basket. Unfortunately, there was really very little worth buying.

There were no passengers for Malta, so the ship went right by it during the night, and we saw nothing. Because of the present tension (*resulting in 1952 Egyptian Revolution*), we will not be able to land at Port Said, but we will have a look around Aden when we arrive. That will be the first port of landing we will have had.

Near Aden, 28 October 1951

Since we wrote last, we have covered quite a bit of territory. When we were approaching the Canal (Suez Canal) we felt quite tense despite all the reassurances. The first indication of Egypt was the appearance of tall palm trees on the beach, and when we were still well out, the ships that had been going through the Mediterranean began to converge, and a small vessel with an Egyptian pilot on board came alongside, and it was not long until we were right in Port Said. It was a lovely sight. We were not allowed to disembark and our captain and an Egyptian police officer had a few heated words of conversation. The captain did not wish anyone to go ashore, and the officer did.

The small boats with their wares soon arrived round the ship and we eventually bought two cotton sun hats for 2/- each. We waited until the ship entered the Canal at 2am. The Canal has to work twenty-four hours per day to keep the shipping from gathering. The pilots on the Canal are French, and there must be quite a French community, for an Egyptian came on board with French newspapers.

Suez was lovely. There were large searchlights, and a loud French voice from a loudspeaker directed the tugs, allowing us to make a slow, steady run through the Canal, with desert on either side, and on through the bitter lakes. There were miles and miles of desert with green patches of irrigation, and there was also the inspiring sight of our "boys" in uniform all the way down in clusters. Banter was exchanged between the soldiers and the passengers, who were shouting: *"Get your knees browned!"*

Unfortunately, the Red Sea has been very uncomfortable, and the least exertion makes us pour with perspiration.

Near Bombay, 3 November 1951

We landed in Aden on Monday and had quite a time going round the shops. There is no purchase tax there, and if you can beat them down in price, you can get a good bargain. Reita got a watch (a Rolex Oyster), which cost £13, but there was not sufficient time to make full use of the cheap shopping.

Dufflaghur Tea Estate, 16 November 1951

When we arrived in Bombay, we got on a train to Calcutta and began a very dreary journey across India. The train was dirty and dusty and there were no beds. We had to sit all the time. People were travelling on the roof and hanging on to the sides of the train, for which reason, there were iron bars across the glassless windows. Beggars sat on the edge of the rail. When we got to Calcutta at 11.30 am on Tuesday, we were very dirty indeed. The countryside in Central India is very desolate, and the rice crop is very poor. To look at rice, it seems almost like wheat, but when we came up to the fertile countryside of Assam, we saw lovely crops. We stayed a few days in Calcutta and had quite a list of shopping to do: wireless set, stores, more light clothing, etc, and at the same time I had to nip round all the firms (Tea) and have a chat with the different people. We stayed at the Grand Hotel, and the Company (Williamson Magor) covered the bill. We left Calcutta on the Friday by air and arrived at our final destination (Dufflaghur Tea Estate) on Sunday.

Dufflaghur Tea Estate, 28 November 1951

We have settled into our bungalow. The roof is of corrugated iron, painted with highly reflecting aluminium paint to reflect the heat. The only alternative is thatch, but owing to the danger of fire, I prefer it as it is. A bungalow in the district with a thatch roof was completely gutted owing to fire.

The wireless we bought in Calcutta has been installed, and we are able to get the News. Short wave listening is not terribly satisfactory, and we have not yet discovered the various wavelengths which change at different times. We do, however, get the BBC News, or Australian, or American. I think the American is relayed from Ceylon. The All-India Programme is not much use, owing to the language, although they have short programmes in English. We also get Radio Moscow very easily, and they give five-minutes propaganda in English, repeating it all afternoon.

We are managing to organise our servants a bit better now. We had great difficulty at first, not knowing a word that was being said. The gardeners (*maalees*) have abandoned the plants in the back garden, and I have not had much time to do anything with them so far. We had thunder and lightning last night with a downpour of rain, but today it is absolutely dry again, although rather cold. We now require a fire in the evening. It is unusual to get rain in any quantity in November.

We had a leopard in the tea garden a few days ago. Someone had stolen its cubs and taken them to a neighbouring tea garden, and the mother returned to our tea garden during the day (unusual) looking for them.

I then got an urgent call to a neighbouring tea garden to see one of the workers. It was a man who had been mauled by a bear. It would appear the bear had come into the tea garden from the jungle during the night and had fallen asleep among the tea bushes. He was literally scalped, and one of his eyes and half of his face had been knocked away. He died this morning.

Dufflaghur Tea Estate, 9 December 1951

Our location is interesting. The foothills of the Himalayas are only three-quarters of a mile from our bungalow, and from there they retreat in ridges of ever-increasing height, until their large peaks (snow-covered) can be seen in the distance. The lower ridges and valleys are covered by jungle and abound with wildlife.

We had a rogue female elephant a few weeks ago. She had become separated from the herd, and came down early, and trampled down the growing paddy (rice), doing a lot of damage to the crop. Food is very scarce for the workforce, and they are dependent wholly on the rice crop. There is a ban on elephant shooting, and special permission to shoot the female rogue had to be obtained from the Assam Provincial Government. One of the keen sportsmen was allocated the task. He was eager to get the rogue, because this would give him the go-ahead to shoot a "tusker" (male) that had been knocking down mud huts by the river, and allow him to keep the tusks.

According to a special order, the Government gets the tusks, unless a female is shot within a short time of killing a male. Something to do with the balance of nature. Unfortunately, when he followed the female two miles into the jungle, he was unable to get a proper shot, and it is dangerous to shoot if you cannot definitely kill. The female disappeared, and has never been seen since: much to the annoyance of the sportsman.

Dufflaghur Tea Estate, 22 December 1951

We have had no rain for a couple of weeks, and everything is becoming very dry and dusty, especially the roads which have no proper tarmac surface. When rain comes during the cold season, it never really amounts to much. During the day, it is quite cold in the bungalow. We keep all the windows and doors open, and have to go out on the lawn to get a heat!

We have been invited by the manager from a neighbouring tea garden to go up river and have a picnic lunch. There appears to be quite a crowd from all the neighbouring tea gardens going there on Christmas Day. Some fish, some swim and others just enjoy the fresh air.

Dufflaghur Tea Estate, 8 January 1952

When we arrived on Christmas Day, there was quite a contingent there. The spot is only just accessible by car, and we landed in a big valley behind the first lot of hills, about seven miles from Dufflaghur.

The Government gives the local tea gardens a small grant to keep this road open. Just beyond this area is political territory, and a special permit is required to go there.

(Mum poses 'up river')

(Dad does a hand-stand)

The water, fresh from the jungle, is clear and unpolluted.

(Dad is to the right in the photo)

There have been no more animal encounters, although when we recounted our experiences to-date to another medical officer's wife, she said she had been in Assam for three years and had seen nothing. Their practice, however, is more in the open, whereas we are right up against the hills and jungle.

We had a day's outing to the big town last Saturday to do some shopping. Tezpur is about eighty-five miles away. The place is not just the best of beauty, although I've no doubt it compares favourably with other parts. The houses, which are mostly mud and bamboo with the occasional corrugated iron roof, are all crowded together, and the streets are full of people, cows, goats, bullock carts and, occasionally, ducks.

In Calcutta, the streets have an abundance of beggars, cripples, etc, in addition, but the roads there are surfaced and the policeman at the corner directs this very varied intermingling of traffic. The taxis in Calcutta are all large American saloons (none in Tezpur), bought from the Yankees at the end of the war (WW2).

This whole area was very active during the war. Supplies sent to China were flown over from India, and in Assam there was an aerodrome every fifty miles, or so, to catch any planes in distress coming back after crossing the mountains. All the troops retreating from Burma (Myanmar) were rescued in Lower Assam, in an exhausted condition, after breaking through miles and miles of jungle.

Before self-rule (1947), all the tea planters (managers, etc) were in the Volunteers, and they did a great deal of work during the war. They would take their labour force away for months at a time into advanced jungle fronts, and build aerodromes, bridges, etc. There is now a small company plane, thirty-five miles away (Bishnauth), which is available for any emergency medical work.

(Aerodrome next to bungalow in Dufflaghur: Mum in middle)

We had quite a quiet time at Christmas and New Year. In this country the younger ones go to the different club parties within a radius of sixty miles, but that would have been too much of an ordeal with so many introductions. We confined ourselves to our own local club (Halem), where we are getting to know all the folks.

We went to a grand dance and party at Hogmanay. This is the annual event here, and our club supplied the visitors for miles around with a nice fish supper (in paper) about 10 pm. At midnight a mock pipe band with paper kilts and all the frills appeared, and to our astonishment, we found it was composed of most of the Englishmen in the district who, by the way, are in the minority.

Dufflaghur Tea Estate, 21 January 1952

We are able to follow the World News on the wireless since we have mastered the various stations and times. Indian standard time is five and a half hours ahead, and we in the tea gardens are a further hour ahead to get the extra time at night.

The bridge between the two parts of my practice will be due to be washed away in another month when the increasing heat liquefies the snow on the mountains.

Our tea garden occupies one thousand acres, of which about six hundred are under tea. It is only a moderately sized garden. The tea is planted out, and the bushes take about four to five years before they are worth very much. Scattered among the bushes are shade trees, which vary in size according to the whim of the agency. These, in addition to providing shade, fix nitrogen from the air, and the leaves provide excellent manure as they fall. The tea, which does so well in the very moist heat, away from the full strength of the sun, is plucked during the hot weather when the growth is active.

(Mum in front of tea bushes)

The best tea, however, is at the beginning and end of the season (slower growth). From the field it is laid out in large storeyed leaf houses to dry, and after reaching a definite stage (about ten days) is put through rollers to burst the individual cells of the leaf, without tearing the leaf (as little as possible, anyway), so that oxidation can take place within the cells. It is then toasted, packed and sent to London, where it is sold in bulk and usually blended after that.

Dufflaghur Tea Estate, 9 February 1952

We were sorry to hear about the King's (George VI) sudden death. Even in India, the post office closed for a day of mourning. Although we settled in very nicely to begin with, the stage of reaction has set in, and at the moment, neither of us could truly say that we are settled. Everything is so different; however, I presume that we are going through the normal human reactions, which will pass off again quite soon.

We have not had long enough to observe the wildlife, and will probably have to get a book to properly appreciate what we are looking for. There are no rabbits, but plenty of hares, which raid the vegetable garden. I have seen a few ponies, but the cow and buffalo are the beasts of burden. A herd of cattle looks very big until you realise that half of them are bulls. The amount of milk given by a cow is very much less than that given by a cow at home, as the animal is only three-quarters the size. Wild dogs prowl round at night, and the wildest is a huge thing with black stripes. We have not heard of any more leopards in the district.

The apple tree will not grow in Assam as it gets confused with the seasons. The winter would suit it fine, but the Monsoon kills it. All the vegetables grown at home do well out here in the winter, but die quickly if planted during the rains. The tea tree is kept very small by constant pruning. They allow it to grow a few inches for a few years until it reaches twenty-eight inches, and then they cut it down to twenty-four inches again. The women do the pruning and the plucking. They are given their correct level, and cut everything away at that level.

At the moment I am trying to catch up with the Government's regulations regarding the welfare of the labour force and the requirements of the Government regarding facilities which should be provided, and on which I have to keep the managers informed. All these regulations were passed during the war years, and are now being brought into force.

Dufflaghur Tea Estate, 24 February 1952

I am preparing the annual reports for the individual tea gardens just now, and this being my first time, and having to rely on the records, I am finding it time-consuming.

On Mondays, I have a spleen muster (*malaria can cause the spleen to become visibly enlarged in children*) in my own area in the morning. The spleen index of the children on a tea garden gives a good idea of the incidence of malaria, and I have been doing these, and anaemic musters, early every morning for the past month.

(Dad at one of the musters)

Paludrine has brought the number of spleens down from 40-60% to 5-15%. A normal haemoglobin (red pigment) out here is 60% as the diet of the labour force is so deficient in protein (not eating meat; and milk, eggs and fish are expensive for them). I have patients with haemoglobin 25%, and although at home this would cause terrific consternation, out here it is quite the routine thing.

Some of the hospitals here are very nice with reasonable facilities and equipment. Most are not just the best as far as cleanliness goes, and patients have to lie on the floor; but it is amazing what one is able to do in the better-equipped ones.

Washing is not a priority, and you find the women beating their clothes on stones in the river to clean them. This is their only way, as soap in any quantity is well out of their budget. When a worker becomes ill, he reports to the hospital, and if necessary, is admitted. The relatives, who come in to make food and attend to sanitary arrangements, etc, do the nursing of the patient.

One gets a great array of clinical material out here that would never be seen in such a short time at home. This week has been one of fractures, the great majority of which we treat on the tea garden, unless they prove to be difficult or complicated.

They are very fond of cock fighting out here, and one man in the hospital had sustained an injury to one of the arteries of his leg (aneurysm) from a deep stab of one of the artificial spurs, which they put on the cocks' legs. As it was nearly at bursting point when I saw him, I decided to operate and tie off the blood vessel. We got him on the table, and with the tourniquet ready to apply, I injected the area with local anaesthetic, and was enlarging the wound, when the aneurysm burst with a spray of blood which drenched me. Fortunately, it was an easy matter to apply the tourniquet and finish the job. He did very well.

Dufflaghur Tea Estate, 13 March 1952

Last weekend we had a thunderstorm with a downpour of rain. The roads which are mostly shingle, or hard-packed earth, became very muddy and difficult to negotiate. The wooden bridges are all being repaired just now, and detours have to be made round them, over ground that is usually almost dry. Unfortunately, the ground on the detours was not packed hard, and after the rain, became so muddy that even the Land Rover had the greatest of difficulty in managing along. On one such day, the road was completely blocked up by a bogged-up lorry on one side, and a bus on the other. I had to turn back and work on a nearer tea garden that day. The next day, however, I did manage to get through.

(Dad and the Land Rover)

The drains through the tea gardens are cut very deep and steep in order to be able to cope with the terrific rush of water during the Monsoon. We are very unlikely to be much affected by major flooding, being so near the foothills. It is in the central plains that the danger occurs mostly. We have had one or two small tremors since we arrived. I have not felt any of them, having either been asleep or outside. Reita felt them in the bungalow, and the fans began to sway quite a bit.

The thunderstorm last weekend seems to be unusual for the time of year, and they were attributing this to the very scanty amount of rain we had at Christmas. It is very obvious when there is going to be rain. The clouds gather for quite a few days beforehand, and it becomes duller and duller, until the lightning starts. The storm is now well away, and the roads are almost as dry as ever. It becomes very pleasant for a few days after the rain to have no clouds of dust flying along the roads with you.

Most of the medical regulations in this part of the world are the fulfilment of acts of Government. They make it compulsory for the Tea Industry to provide various services to the labour forces: medical, holidays, fasting, etc, more or less as at home. Although these acts were passed before and during the war, it is only now that full pressure is being made to bear on these problems.

The import duty on any article of machinery, which would save manpower, is prohibitive, so there will always be work available. The food problem for the worker is very great, and in order to be able to keep a labour force, the tea garden buys rice, etc, and sells it to them at a loss. Since the rice shortage, wheat products have been substituted, much to the consternation of the workers, and the Government started an allocation scheme so that everyone would have a fair ration. Unfortunately, they were not always able to have rice to allocate, and it was very difficult to explain this to the labour force.

It is very interesting to be out here and see the ways of the people. The bird life and plant life offer plenty of scope, but I have plenty on my hands at the moment, learning the language and adapting myself. After a year, when I've caught up with everything, I think life should prove more interesting and relaxing.

Dufflaghur Tea Estate, 17 March 1952

I have had quite a hectic time since I started this letter on 13 March. Firstly, I had to complete a medical examination of a new member of staff, following concerns raised by other staff members. He, unfortunately, had not been properly vetted, and was not terribly good from a psychiatric point of view.

Next, I got a call to the other end of the district (thirty-five, or, forty miles) in the early hours of Saturday morning, and had to return again during the day. This was to deal with a European case of tuberculosis. The patient was at that time in rather a weak state owing to haemoptysis (coughing of blood). I am hoping to get her to Calcutta or Shillong this week.

Then last night, I had another night call in my own district to see the wife of one of the Indian staff who was suffering from acute intestinal obstruction, due to adhesions from a previous intra-abdominal suppurative condition, for which I treated her about three weeks ago. She delivered unto herself a son at that time, with peritonitis at the same time. She would not go into hospital, but did quite well with sulphonamides, penicillin and chloromycetin, until this obstruction developed.

Lastly, I had a suspected case of smallpox today. The rash is not completely out yet, but we will see what it definitely is by tomorrow. I have got one of the AMOs (assistant medical officers) busy vaccinating all the contacts, to be on the safe side. There are usually a few cases now and then, but this will be my first if it does happen to be one.

Sending a patient to one of the big hospitals (mission hospitals) means around twelve hours on the night steamer, up and across the river.

The Europeans have the privilege of taking the small plane, which is becoming very popular on the tea gardens in Assam. They are cheaper than the expensive cars, working out about £1,000; but unless the manager has an expert knowledge of the servicing, he is taking quite a risk. The normal flying hours of one of these planes works out at a little over ten, each week.

Dufflaghur Tea Estate, 12 April 1952

The case of smallpox, which I mentioned in my last letter, died on the fifteenth day of illness with hypostatic pneumonia. After the first week of illness, when in a confused state, the patient decided to get his bow and arrows, and go hunting for birds, and was out of isolation for three to four hours. His particular class are very keen on hunting, and they make very effective bows and arrows from springy bamboo. They fix a metal spear point to the arrow, and are occasionally able to shoot even a leopard. They are particularly keen on the wild fowl in the jungle. Fortunately, no one was infected, and the isolation system seems to have been satisfactory, as there have been no new cases. The whole labour force of the garden (about two thousand) was vaccinated after receiving an urgent supply of lymph from Shillong.

The weather remains very hot and dry, and they say the water in the rivers is beginning to rise, but I haven't, so far, noticed much difference. The next dollop of rain should cool things a bit, and still the dust. We will probably lose the wooden bridge (over the Boroi River) in a month or so. This connects the two parts of my practice.

I attended someone about three weeks ago. He had been mauled by a bear while hunting in the jungle. The bear, fortunately, had come up from the rear, and although the man's ribs were slightly exposed at some parts with the blows of the bear, no vital damage was done, and he has recovered very quickly.

We lost one of our bearers (personal servant) a week ago. He was a young fellow, and very good. However, he decided to fall in love with another man's wife, and as the other chap was understandably not very pleased, and was a bit heftier than the bearer, the pair decided to elope. I have heard nothing of them since. Reita decided to promote one of the *pani-wallahs* (washing up boys), and he is certainly putting on a good show. We got servants' clothes from Calcutta, as is customary, and are now wondering how to get the new bearer squeezed into the set of the previous bearer, who was a very small chap!

Time is flying past very quickly. I feel I have very few spare minutes. We are feeling quite settled now, but get homesick occasionally. We have no difficulty in making ourselves understood now with the servants, and by the time we have been here a year, we should have a fair grasp of the language.

I had my first case of a snake bite in the district a few days ago. The patient, who was working among the tea, suddenly appeared at the hospital in the manager's car. I quickly applied a tourniquet above the site to prevent absorption of poison, and gave the antivenom serum intravenously. The tourniquet can only be left on for half an hour, and as the patient was still free of symptoms at that time, I can only presume that it was a non-poisonous snake. The recent heat has been bringing them out of hibernation. Since the teeth marks were about half an inch to three-quarters of an inch apart, it must have been quite a big snake.

Tonight is the night for the Hindi film in the tea garden, and the servants were very keen to get finished quickly. The film is shown in the open air. All the tea gardens own a projector between them, and show a film to the labour force about once a month. Our club (Halem) borrows the machine, so we also get films about once a month. Some of the films are in English, as Hindi ones are not always available. When this happens, we pop over to see them. The last one was *King Kong*, and it was as old as the hills! This evening, the *chowkidar* (night watchman) did not want to go, and got the job of bringing in our after-dinner tea at 9 pm. We are getting used to him during the night. To begin with we found it difficult to sleep owing to the sound of his snoring as he guarded our bungalow!

Dufflaghur Tea Estate, 4 May 1952

I am among the annual reports, which should have been written ages ago, but with my limited appreciation of local conditions, it was as well to wait. The river between the two parts of my practice, is still manageable. The bridge, which has felt the strain following the recent thunderstorms, is tottering, and in a few weeks, it will be washed away. It is made entirely of bamboo, yet it can still take buses and lorries. It is about seventy yards in length, and they continuously have to reinforce the bamboo supports. Once the bridge goes, I will have to cross by ferry boat, and owing to the trouble involved with that, I will not be taking too many unnecessary journeys.

When I first saw the ferry, I thought it could not possibly take a car over, but it does: and two at a time, one of them often being a bus or lorry. It is comprised of two very deep wide canoes, with a platform between them, and is propelled by large poles. It will be November before a new (temporary) bridge can again be built.

(Ferry in background carrying passengers)

(Bus being transported, then driving away on the other side)

I was called in to see a man, following an accident in the factory yesterday.

(Factory is behind the trees)

There is a large master driving rod in all the factories, with varying sizes of driving wheels, at regular intervals, to accommodate belts which divide the various pieces of machinery. The engines vary between 100 and 150 HP in the various factories. This man had been handling a belt which was hanging over the driving rod, next to the wheel.

It was not driving, as it was disconnected from the sugar cane crushing machine. He had fallen in some way, and tightened the belt, which immediately took grip of the driving rod and carried him up to a height of about ten feet. He then managed to get his arm round the driving rod, and was rotated round with it, until his arm parted company with him, and he fell to the floor, leaving his arm on the machinery.

The arm had been fractured in its middle third, and the muscles torn off, leaving about three inches of exposed bone. The brachial artery had been stripped, and owing to its elasticity, had curled and made the control of haemorrhage easy.

I took the temporary dressing off this morning, and redressed it.

Owing to gas gangrene infection, I have made no endeavour, as yet, to attend to bone, or close the wound. I have put him on a huge dose of penicillin, which should kill the gas gangrene, after which, we will be able to attend to the stump. The artery looked very precarious in any case, and even a small haemorrhage would have weighed the balance. I will let you know next time how he is getting on.

My cars are running quite well at the moment. I have a driver to attend to the details, and he is very good. He takes away my personal interest in the cars. Every other week, however, I inspect them on the ramp to see that everything looks adequately serviced. I have taken a few more photographs, and will let you have copies quite soon.

Meantime, I have enclosed a copy of our staff. They are, from left to right:

1. First bearer (the one that fell in love with another fellow's wife, and ran off with her, disappearing, since the former husband was a big tough fellow, and the couple were afraid).

2. Pani-Wallah (the one that replaced the first bearer, but is now the second bearer in the dining room.) As the Pani-Wallah, he did the washing up. He is doing quite well in his new job.

3. Sweeper (he does all the floors in the bungalow, washing and odd jobs).

4. Cook's Pani-Wallah (he used to do the washing up in the cookhouse, which is a separate building from the bungalow, and where all the cooking is done under very primitive conditions. He would carry the water (pani) from the well. The water is brown, and is boiled and kept in the fridge. He has now been promoted to "Bottle Washer Khana Pani-Wallah", and assists the second bearer at dinner.

5. Temporary driver, when my own one was away.

6. Cook.

7. Original second bearer (he is now the first bearer, and attends to the bedroom, clothes, etc).

8. Sitting down are the two maalees (gardeners).

The night watchman (*chowkidar*) is not there. He is the one that keeps us awake at night with his snoring. He will be away ploughing his rice land. Most of the servants are Hindus, but the cook is a Buddhist.

Dufflaghur Tea Estate, 9 May 1952

I had a cat to attend to yesterday. It was only three-quarters grown, but was delivering kittens. After three days in labour, it had delivered a breech to the head, but the head had got stuck, and someone had managed to drag it out. The next kitten, a vertex presentation (head first) was completely stuck. It had a huge head, and I had a good laugh to myself as I delivered it with ovum forceps (normally used for removing aborted material), which fitted the head very well. On palpation of the abdomen, I could feel another kitten (a breech). She will manage to deliver this one as far as the head, and then someone can pull it out like the first one.

Dufflaghur Tea Estate, 6 June 1952

Our back garden is now empty. All the winter vegetables are finished and the tropical stuff is not ready. We have two small banana trees, which will take a couple of years to grow, and a patch of pineapples, which will not be ready until nearer the end of the hot season. I have plans to get more banana tree cuttings planted.

The oranges out here are like tangerines, but I will find out the procedure and get some planted. Grapes grow well, and also a fruit tree called a lychee. I don't know what this tree is like, but the fruit is lovely. It is half grape and half plum, and really delicious. We have kept the large central stones of some that were given to us, and will try to get seedlings.

Foot and mouth disease seems to be endemic in India. They take it for granted that there will be an outbreak every few years, but here the death rate seems to be small. The cows could hardly give less milk than they do at present, and it is quite a common thing to see a dead cow by the roadside being consumed by vultures. These fellows are like big turkeys, and go red in the face as they gobble over a large piece of flesh. Their resistance to disease must be exceedingly high. On the wing, they are slow, clumsy birds.

We have quite a few hawks, bigger than the ones at home, and almost identical in shape. I think I saw a large flock of swifts last week. They were like swallows, but much smaller than the ones at home. There were none here all winter, and I was presuming they were coming from the south of India to nest here, or in the foothills. There are other brightly coloured birds to be seen now and then. We last saw monkeys at the jungle picnic place more than a month ago, when they threw things from the trees at our Land Rover.

One of the workers was slightly mauled by a leopard on the tea garden last week, not two hundred yards from our bungalow. It had fallen asleep after some night prowling, and was disturbed by the tea pluckers. It has not reappeared since, and has probably changed its "digs"! We are getting used to this sort of thing. One of the beasts that is really feared is the bear, as it always makes a mess of anyone whom it mauls. Some of the frogs (hundreds of them) are very big, and make a terrific noise at night, croaking in chorus. The mosquitoes are on the prowl, but have not reached their worst yet.

I was out during Friday night at a tea garden (Behali Tea Estate) about ten miles away, attending to a labour case (the wife of one of the Indian staff). She was suffering from obstructed labour: her eighth baby. I stayed for three-quarters of an hour, but did not do anything, as she was not ready. However, I got the head turned, and the baby delivered by forceps at midday yesterday, after the manager came for me by car. He told me they were in a terrible state of emotional unrest, and could not be consoled. I have seen her since, and the mother and baby daughter are doing very well.

The number of obstructed labours out here is much less in proportion to population at home, as the babies are almost all premature, and very small. I see something out of the usual almost every other day. The tea garden I attended on Friday is the biggest in my district, and plans are going ahead for the construction of a maternity unit there. The plans have all been made to suit my suggestions, and it will give me great satisfaction to get this into proper working order, after it has been built. This should be done next cold weather.

I sent the fellow, who had his arm torn off in the factory, to the Jorhat Mission Hospital, as his condition was poor. I have not heard how he is getting on, but he should be all right. I have had two liver abscesses in the last two weeks: both men, and not very old. One died two hours after admission to hospital, and I did not see him until after death. The other was lying in hospital for five days (of which I was unaware) before I saw him during my routine visit. I operated under local anaesthesia, and inserted a drainage tube. About one and a half pints of pus were removed. Unfortunately, his condition had deteriorated too far, and he died the same evening. I am past being annoyed at this sort of thing.

Dufflaghur Tea Estate, 27 June 1952

The insects are now out in full force, but we take our paludrine regularly, and should not have any trouble with malaria. There is a lot of malaria in the hospitals just now. The sickness rates are very high on all the tea gardens. Respiratory infections (coryza, bronchitis, influenza, pneumonia, etc) form the bulk of it at the moment. A near second are bowel infections (diarrhoea, enteritis, dysenteries, etc). These latter are an indication of standards of sanitation. I have had a few sporadic cases of paratyphoid, but none of the full-blown thing.

There were no more cases of smallpox, and the climate is now not very suitable for spread of the disease. However, I see in the Calcutta newspaper that there has been a disastrous outbreak among the hill-tribes of the Naga Hills. They will be pleased to see the Monsoon. It shows the value of regular vaccination.

I have a patient at the moment with a liver abscess. I have already drained two pockets of pus from her liver, but feel that she has another abscess forming in a different part of her liver. She came in at first with a severe pneumonia, and developed one abscess, which I drained between the ribs. The liver continued to enlarge, and I drained a further one with an upper abdominal incision two weeks ago.

She improved greatly after that, but her liver has started to enlarge again, and her heart is beginning to fail. Her general condition was so poor yesterday when I saw her, that I decided to do nothing. She will probably die, as she cannot possibly stand much more of this sort of thing. There has been so much pus that I doubt there is much healthy liver tissue left. A portable X-ray would be just the thing for letting me know where, and how many abscesses are present. I will let you know what happens.

There was a case of rabies at one of the hospitals a few weeks ago. The patient died shortly after admission, however, before I had time to see him. I have not yet seen a case of rabies. We get the occasional case of tetanus every now and then, and very often in new-born infants. It is the custom with some of the classes to dress the navel with cow dung, and what could be asking for it more?

We get a few cases of eclampsia. I was called to see a case three weeks ago. The patient had been having convulsions, and was in a coma all day in her house, before medical aid was sought. She was ready for instruments when I saw her, and after being put under with chloroform, I applied the forceps and started gentle traction. I was able to do absolutely nothing. When I measured the outlet of her bony pelvis, the shortest measurement was two and a half inches.

Almost all of the infants are premature (anything from two and a half pounds to five pounds), so usually little difficulty is encountered. In this case, it was just too much. I had eventually to perforate the head of the infant in order to deliver her, and stop her having fits.

Since this incident, we have been getting the mothers to come into hospital to have their babies, under proper supervision. They are too fond of getting some old woman in to deliver their babies, and this affects the stillbirth and maternal mortality rates, which are prevailing.

By next cold weather, I now hope to have three maternity hospitals up and running, and have every normal case supervised by the trained midwife. These midwives are usually given a year's course of instruction at one of the mission hospitals, after which, they get a diploma. Given a proper chance, their results are really very good, and you can always be sure of a timely warning from them if anything goes wrong.

Dufflaghur Tea Estate, 23 July 1952

I seem to have been kept on the hop since I started this letter. I do not know whether the newspapers will have had anything in them about floods and earthquakes. There was a tremor at Tezpur about a week ago, but of no severity. Some parts of Assam have had very damaging floods. Our rivers were certainly very wild, but too near the hills to have much chance of changing course, as they do in other parts.

The mails have been held up considerably, and we have not had your papers for a fortnight. No doubt they will all arrive in a bunch. I have arranged with Halem Tea Estate to send two pounds of tea every month to you, in single containers. The three-pound box requires a special licence, which has now been suspended.

Dufflaghur Tea Estate, 4 August 1952

It is almost impossible to believe it is now August. The seasons are so different. We have had quite a bit of heat, but not so much regular rain. The managers are complaining that it is not coming regularly enough. We get a terrific downpour, and then that really hot sun comes out again. The river has been giving quite a bit of trouble since the earthquakes, and has constantly been changing course: even more than usual. It is now about two or three miles wide with sandbags at regular intervals, and so shallow in parts, with the constant deposit of silt, that the steamers get grounded every now and then.

I had to do an amputation (mid-thigh), yesterday, for sarcoma.

Reita came down to hand out instruments.

One of the AMOs (Dr Babu) and I amputated the limb. It was fortunate that it occurred on a tea garden where the medical staff are young and helpful. Dr Babu, although very junior in service, is the most mentally active that I have in the district. The whole thing went like clockwork, with spinal anaesthesia: although, during the operation, one of the ligatures slipped, and we had to take very quick and energetic measures to prevent bleeding.

When I saw the patient today, she was satisfactory. The bone marrow, however, above the amputation site was invaded by malignant growth, so the outlook is hopeless in any case. I wanted her to have the operation six weeks ago, but she and her family could not be convinced that it was so serious.

Dufflaghur Tea Estate, 23 August 1952

The mails in Assam have been very upset since the flooding, and I hope you are getting our letters. At the moment I am reading the latest on malaria prophylaxis so I can give the Company (Williamson Magor) a considered answer to a recent letter. There is no doubt that paludrine has not been the success that was initially promised, and the recent new antimalarial drugs are more expensive (chloroquine, camoquin, daraprim, etc). I have been wading through pages and pages of this stuff to get the most accurate, present-day opinion.

I have had one or two wee tiffs with some of the managers. They can be very exasperating. Each has his own wee area, where his say is law, and sometimes they like to extend their orders to the visiting medical officer. Still, there is talk of us getting a portable X-ray in this district.

Dufflaghur Tea Estate, 18 September 1952

Since the fall in the price of tea, I have been answering letters from Williamson Magor regarding proposed cuts in hospital development. I no sooner get one lot cleared, when another lot arrives.

The last fortnight has been very wet, but we are always pleased to see the rain to bring down the temperature. Another month will see a marked change in the season. At the present moment, the roads are flooded with water, but this will clear quickly. They have finished planting the rice (all by hand), and by the time it has a month of heat and rain, it will have had a good start. When the fields go dry, it looks more like a crop of wheat than anything else.

I saw a very large cobra on the road today. A lorry was coming in the opposite direction, and when the driver saw it, he swerved the lorry, and ran over it. He then stopped and backed over it again. Despite that, it managed to crawl away into the long grass. It was waving its head during this process, and I did not leave the car to investigate. It would have been about six to seven feet long. There are not very many of these fellows going about here.

Dufflaghur Tea Estate, 19 September 1952

It is now more than a year since we left Falkirk, and it has been the shortest year I have known. We are in really good form, and well acclimatised now. We take a small paludrine tablet every day to keep the malaria parasites at bay. I am pretty well versed in all the tropical conditions, and find that most of the illness is due to conditions that could quite easily occur at home. Unfortunately, I do not have Falkirk Royal Infirmary to help me out, as I used to have, and have to set all the fractures, etc, unless there are special complications, when I send them by river steamer to the Mission Hospital on the south bank of the Brahmaputra: the journey being from twelve to sixteen hours away.

The AMOs are very helpful, and handle all the routine coughs and colds, pneumonias, etc, without any difficulty. They have a licentiate degree, following a four-year course, which qualifies them for such work. The Calcutta M.B., B.S. is equivalent to our own degree, and is recognised in the UK as such. Unfortunately, owing to the amount of British capital in Tea, there are not very many Indian doctors in the Industry.

There was an outbreak of rinderpest at Halem, a few weeks ago. I had a good look at all the animals, and now have a good book on the pathology of the cow. I am really quite interested in this animal, and hope we will be able to have some within a few months. The only drawback is: who will do the milking?

Dufflaghur Tea Estate, 30 September 1952

We had a tiger outside our window two nights ago: fierce, growling. All our windows were wide open and only covered with mosquito wire. We were quite pleased when he departed, and it did not take me long to fix the windows in an almost closed position. I might add that during the tiger's visit, our night watchman, who was on the veranda at the time, slept peacefully like a baby.

There has not been a great deal of animal life, recently. Tigers very seldom go into the mud and bamboo houses, and the Indian is perfectly confident that they will not do this. Now and again, however, they run away with a cow, or a dog, and it seems to be a well-known fact that the tiger is fond of a "doggy breakfast".

The harvest celebrations have just finished. All the rice has been planted and the rain will not be very heavy now. In a couple of weeks, it will be completely finished. The nights are quite cool, but we haven't stopped using the fan, yet.

The Tea Industry is hoping for the finish of rationing. There is now a glut, and the prices do not always clear the cost of manufacture. Some of the tea gardens in Darjeeling have already closed down as there is no demand for quality tea. The public only wants cups to the packet. Cuts in tea garden expenses are being made everywhere, and medical development plans are being temporarily abandoned.

Dufflaghur Tea Estate, 1 October 1952

I wrote my agents a very long letter regarding malaria in the district, ten days ago. I covered absolutely every aspect of it. It took me a month to think about, collect statistics and write. However, they thanked me profusely for it.

Dufflaghur Tea Estate, 22 October 1952

Our servants keep us on our toes. On Monday, one of the bearers was on leave, and the other one arrived to serve dinner in an inebriated condition. I had to give him medication to sober him up! A few days later, Reita discovered that her salt and pepper dishes were broken (two chickens with holes in the head). When she enquired as to the cause, it was carefully explained that the hens had come in, and being attracted to them, broke them. It is usually the cat that gets the blame: only we don't have one!

We have had an exceptional amount of rain in the first half of this month, but the heavy rain is now more or less finished. The river (Boroi) which I cross on Mondays and Tuesdays, is now much better, and will not give me too much bother. The temporary bridge (bamboo) will be completed by the end of November. Plans for a permanent bridge have been passed by the Central Government at the cost of Rupees 16 lakhs (£120,000). Work is starting in the cold weather of 1953.

The water table in the garden was up to two inches from the surface, until recently. We have a small first batch of vegetables sown (turnips, carrots, etc), and some cabbages and cauliflowers planted out from boxes on the veranda. All the plants must be planted early in the morning, or in the evening, owing to the strong sun. Small shades have to be slanted over them. A banana tree gives suitable pieces of bark, which can be cut to suit. We hope to have some flowers planted by next week.

Dufflaghur Tea Estate, 4 November 1952

Reita and I did another amputation operation, a few days ago, for gangrene of foot. Things went off very well, and the patient (quite a young man, about forty years, with degenerative changes in the arteries of his right leg), is now doing fine.

I took the leg off just above the knee, and when I examined the popliteal artery (behind the knee) after the operation, it was thickened to such an extent, that only a fine point could get into the lumen (channel in the centre). We will get some sort of artificial limb made on the tea garden, and he will be fit as a night watchman.

During the operation, a fly, which had managed to get into theatre, landed on my back, and the compounder (pharmacist), no doubt thinking about germs, gave me a clatter on the back to kill it. No thanks to him that I didn't start amputating the other limb! However, I was ready to close the wound by that time.

The girl who had amputation for sarcoma of leg, is now doing well, and her haemoglobin has come up. She had rather a sticky course. It is to be hoped that there are no more malignant seedlings in other parts of the body, but she will be most fortunate if there are not. She was riddled with malaria at the same time, but her spleen and liver, etc, are now normal. I had wondered, at the time, if the enlarged liver might be an early secondary.

Dufflaghur Tea Estate, 17 November 1952

There are quite a few cases of malaria (relapses) just now, with the sudden change in the weather. It has become chilly in the evening, and we are almost ready to light a fire. The cook had a temperature of one hundred and three degrees Fahrenheit, last night, but after some chloroquine (new treatment), his temperature rapidly fell, although he still looks a bit seedy. He has been taking it very easy today.

I developed a very nasty "cold" myself, about ten days ago, and succeeded in getting my sinuses clogged up. They are beginning to clear now, but I have developed a cough at night. Although full of complaints (Reita says) I have not been fevered, or off work, but most of the European staff have been down with flu.

I have a lot of letters that keep coming in, and were piling up while I had the "cold". I am determined to get my letters written tonight.

Dufflaghur Tea Estate, 21 December 1952

I have not gone out to work this morning. I have decided to catch up with all the clerical work that has accumulated. Reita is away to the Halem Club to do a wee bit in preparation for a Christmas party. The children in the district, and the neighbouring one, are all coming to it. No energy has been spared to make this a success. So far as I understand, all the adults will be in attendance as well to watch the antics of Santa, who is arriving by elephant to distribute presents. One of the young fellows in the district will be dressed as Santa, and we are all hoping he does not fall off the elephant's back!

Dufflaghur Tea Estate, 11 January 1953

I have been making good use of a book on tropical medicine: *Synopsis of Tropical Medicine*. I am getting very interested in malnutrition and all the deficiency states. My biggest headache at the moment is trying to reduce the drug bill without upsetting treatment. I need to cut out the delicacies of treatment, the value of which is doubtful, or temporary, and I have spent weeks on this.

A fortnight or so ago, two brothers from the labour force decided to have a row after getting drunk. One fellow made fifteen lacerations on the other with a pruning knife. When I saw him, the AMO had already inserted fifty stitches to various parts of his body, but mainly the head and face. He could not, however, cope with the left wrist and forearm, which were almost severed in two, and had to have a tourniquet on continuously. We amputated the arm above the elbow that evening without any hitches, and he is doing very well.

Dufflaghur Tea Estate, 21 January 1953

We have not seen any wild animals for a long time now, but the neighbouring tea garden lost two cows during the day about three weeks ago. It must have been a hungry tiger, for a leopard seldom comes out to hunt during the day. It would appear the herdsmen were taking all the cows to new pastures, and two wandered into the jungle. Since the cows are very small, a tiger can carry one away without any bother.

The scarcity of grass is always very acute during the cold weather, and the cows gradually become skin and bone. There is no question of winter feeding, as this would deprive the people. The reason for grass scarcity is the lack of rain, with the relatively strong sun, which burns everything up. If some of the rainfall could be spread over the cold season, this would be one of the most productive areas in the world.

I have a new driver. He is doing quite well at the moment, but has no licence, yet. He is very willing and level-headed. He does the work on the vehicles, while I read him instructions from the service manual. He was driving a lorry on the tea garden previously, but has been working with vehicles for the last eight or so years. He was born on Halem Tea Estate, and must be about thirty years old. Most of the workers do not know their exact ages. He does my "on-garden" driving, and is well experienced. When he went for his test at the police station for his lorry licence this month, he was failed because he did not know the road signs, and no one had gone over them with him beforehand. He has to wait another six months before the inspector comes round again. In any case, you would have to go some distance up the bank of the Brahmaputra before seeing any of the road signs on the test charts. They are mostly different from the ones at home, and there are many more to cope with the almost complete illiteracy of the drivers in this part of the world.

The sickness rates in the hospitals are very low just now. This is the healthy part of the year. I am still doing the survey of medical costs to see if economies can be made. The bill for last year was Rs 60,000 to Rs 70,000 (roughly £5,000) for the district as a whole, and was even greater the previous year. It is a big job pricing the medicines to see which are the luxuries, and which are not. I am trying to find which preparations are the best buy, and the differences in the prices of similar products out here, are really terrific. Luminal (phenobarbitone made by Bayer) costs Rs 16 per ounce. Gardenal (phenobarbitone made by M&B) costs Rs 4 per ounce. You can see the difficulties involved when you consider that these two preparations are equally effective in treatment.

Dufflaghur Tea Estate, 25 January 1953

I had a call to Halem Tea Garden in the early hours of Thursday morning. Two young fellows from the Halem work force had been coming back from fishing (so they say), when they met a Punjabi and two others (all drunk) from the village. They exchanged some rude remarks, and when I saw one of the young fellows, he had a stab wound (from below, upwards) in the centre of his abdomen, and four feet of intestine prolapsing through the wound.

I cleaned the grass and twigs off his intestine, and returned it to the abdomen, after repairing the perforation. He also had another stab wound below the heart, with a shattered rib, and extensive internal bleeding. I tried to patch him up, but it was hopeless, and he died the next morning from exsanguinations. He and his brother had been up to no good during the night, and had got more than they bargained for.

This tea garden has had three or four murders in the last few years: mostly the result of drink, which is illegally brewed in the villages. The police raid the producers every now and then, but a fine of Rs 1,000 means nothing to them.

I have never seen a bear, only the result of an attack. They are fickle creatures, and their aggressiveness is due to fear. The most feared of the animals, nevertheless, is the wild elephant that can turn a car over and trample it to bits.

One of the tea planters was telling us that when he first came out, he had an old car that gave him a lot of problems starting. On one such occasion he was returning from a shooting expedition, and was trying (with difficulty) to start the car, when an elephant came on to the jungle road, and charged him. The elephant gave the car such a dunt at the back (it was in gear), that the car started, and went flying down the road to safety. He was afraid to tell his wife of the incident in case she stopped him going on shooting expeditions, and the first she heard of it was in the Calcutta Office about a year later: much to her surprise and dismay.

Dufflaghur Tea Estate, 8 February 1953

The manager of the neighbouring garden saw an elephant crossing the river where we have our picnics. He was worried at first, in case it might be frightened and attack him, but it just lifted its trunk, snorted and went on its merry way.

Everyone has a healthy respect for the wild elephant. It can catch a tiger with its trunk, and crash it to the ground, but tears in its hide made by tigers are very liable to go septic and produce serious wounds. When you pass a domesticated elephant on the road, it usually turns to face you until your car passes. One of the hunters in the district, who goes into the jungle frequently to hunt, tells the story of a bull elephant that charged his elephant. His got down on its knees, and took the impact straight on. There was a shudder, and the wild bull bounced back to the side with a broken neck.

The wooden bridges on the roads are being repaired for the 1953 Monsoon. Recently, the Public Ways Department has put a scheme under way to divert a river into a different drainage area. This will bring a considerable amount of extra water under and over my outlet road. Last year, without the extra water, there were days when the water came right up to the level of one particular bridge, but did not go any further because it had already washed the road away on either side, and this formed a safety valve. This year they have brought the road up a level, and with the extra water this bridge is sure to go. I will have to try and find a way out through the other garden, which is relieved of the water.

Dufflaghur Tea Estate, 30 March 1953

We have had the most unusual weather this year. The roads are usually dry and very dusty, at this time, but not this year. Can you imagine our plight? I have been careful in avoiding the possibility of getting stuck in the mud. I did not manage to get to the other end of my practice today, but got an urgent call to a more accessible part. The ruts on the road are anything up to a foot deep. However, one day of strong sun is like a magic wand to the mud.

We have been going to the picnic place every week, but have not always been successful. One week, it rained so hard, that we were soaked to the skin. This did not prevent us from bathing in the middle of it all.

Our journey to the jungle is one of the things that keeps one week from slipping into the next.

Our films (once a fortnight now) also help. We are due one on Saturday, if the mail bus manages to get through.

We are almost halfway through our contract. The rumour goes that if you renew it, the remuneration is much increased, but I suppose that will depend to some extent on the price of tea. They are cutting expenses right, left and centre in the Industry, but the prices have recently shown some slight improvement. This part of Assam, which was most recently converted from jungle to tea, is not as badly hit as other parts, where the bushes are longer in the tooth, and the soil is less helpful.

The mosquitoes are out in force again, and antimalarial measures are again active. We still dabble away with our paludrine, and have very good health: touch wood. I am collecting data and statistics for the various annual health reports at the moment. I hope to complete them within a month this year. It was terrible last year. I had only been in the district for two months of 1951, and knew nothing of the local conditions. I completed the last one for 1951 in

September 1952, and was told afterwards, that I was not really expected to do them for 1951.

Dufflaghur Tea Estate, 16 April 1953

We are getting into the heat now. Fans are going, and the insects (big ones and wee ones), are out in style again. The fan sprays them all over the room. It is almost eighteen months since we arrived in Assam, and we will not be sorry to see our leave time approaching.

Dufflaghur Tea Estate, 1 May 1953

The heat is really making its presence known. The maximum here is ninety degrees Fahrenheit. Two weeks ago, in Calcutta, it was one hundred and eight degrees Fahrenheit. We had the ICI representative from Calcutta for lunch ten days ago, and he said every blow of wind was roasting hot.

Dufflaghur Tea Estate, 11 May 1953

The old Land Rover keeps going despite everything. We went up the jungle river yesterday, as this will probably be our last chance, since the small (road) bridges are getting washed away.

I crossed the bamboo bridge (over the River Boroi) today after the rain. It is on its last legs. I would not be surprised if it has been breached by tomorrow morning. After that, it takes about seven to ten days for them to get the ferry running.

I've recently done a comprehensive analysis of the various prophylactics in malaria control, and have written my findings regarding circumstances, as they are in this district, in a circular to the Agents (Williamson Magor) and the Assam Branch of the Ross Institute of Tropical Diseases.

Malaria transmission is quite different in different parts of the world and different localities. The modern potent antimalarial drugs (chloroquine, camoquin, daraprim, etc) are very expensive, and, therefore, not suitable for mass prophylaxis, like paludrine, which last, unfortunately, has a number of drawbacks.

Some of the hospitals here are good, whereas others are a bit dilapidated. One or two of my AMOs are very good, but others are practising medicine of twenty years ago. I was surprised at some of the drugs. Some had been discarded as useless years previously. I am trying to make them aware that medical treatment is undergoing a revolution (a big one too) at the present moment. The advances in every field are terrific.

This whole area of mine is very highly malarious (or was) in its foothill situation. The particular mosquito that carries 98% of the malaria here, does not lay eggs in dirty pools, only in clean slowly running water with grassy verges (rivers, streams and very occasionally, rice land).

Dufflaghur Tea Estate, 1 June 1953

I have been very busy on malaria statistics, still trying to see which methods are giving the best results at the most economical cost. Dr Gilroy of the Ross Institute has now contacted me, and has asked me to write an article for the India and Pakistan Branch Annual Report. He is going home shortly, and will bring Professor Macdonald from the London Headquarters of the Institute back with him for a cold weather tour of Assam. Both will pay us a visit.

No one could have been more amazed than I was when the letter arrived. Professor Macdonald was for many years in Assam as a younger man, but now has his headquarters at London University for the branches all over the world. He did the WHO (World Health Organisation) report on malaria conditions in Korea last year, and incidentally, was the man who interviewed me for my present job.

The Indian Tea Association (ITA) pays a regular subscription to the Ross Institute for advice on all matters concerning tropical health. In fact, most of the Assam research is done through the Institute.

The time has passed very quickly in Assam, and I have never had a minute without needing to do something. Reita has been very good despite the long hours she has had to spend alone. She always finds something to do. She takes to do with the servants, and the bungalow seems to look after itself as far as I am concerned. There are a further seventeen months to go before I complete my contract; after that, I will tell you what we are going to do.

Dufflaghur Tea Estate, 24 June 1953

We were very pleased to hear that your Coronation celebrations ran according to plan. Our own celebrations at the Bishnauth Club went well. The folks put a considerable amount of work into the preparations, and were rewarded by the pleasure obtained by everyone. One of the activities, in particular, was very good. There was a long piece of bare copper wire, which was twisted into all sorts of shapes, and you had to slip a small loop along it, without touching it, otherwise about half a dozen especially noisy horns were set off, at the same time, by an electric current, as soon as the wires touched. I was fascinated by the whole thing, and was among the few people to win a prize, which turned out to be some old tins from the club store that they wanted to get rid of!

We have been leading a very quiet life since then in isolation. The Boroi Bridge was washed away in the middle of May, and I have been fiddling about in small boats every Monday and Tuesday since then. The delays can be innumerable and the constancy of it all is very apt to annoy you when you see everyone fiddling about. No one seems to know the meaning of speed.

We have been very lucky with the heat this year: either that, or we are getting used to it. We make a point of avoiding undue exposure to sunlight, whenever possible. Reita, at any rate, is doing much better this year than last, and apart from a few scorching days, I have not felt uncomfortable at all.

The Monsoon has now broken properly with grey rainy days and thunderstorms. It is lovely to hear the rain and feel the temperature drop. The rain we had earlier in the year was due to a fault in the winds over Bengal. The moisture-laden wind from the Bay of Bengal did not drop its rain because the western component was not strong enough this year (from the opposite direction) to make it do so. All the rain went straight on to Assam (foothills), and almost drowned us out. The Monsoon, however, has now reached us normally, and apart from being about thirty inches of rain ahead of schedule, all is well. East Bengal, in particular, had quite a severe drought before the Monsoon arrived.

We were delighted about the results of the Everest expedition, especially when the rumours of failure owing to the coding system came out first. It was a pity that some of the less honest types out here decided to distort the facts.

Dufflaghur Tea Estate, 15 July 1953

We had intended to make the journey to Tezpur today. One of the assistant managers in the district took a very bad attack of malaria, following influenza, about three weeks ago. He is not a young man: over fifty. His condition was very weak, and his heart not too good, afterwards. I had arranged for him to fly to Calcutta from Tezpur for special investigations, and was going to take him in my Land Rover. Unfortunately, the rain has been so heavy, and the river so high and rough, that it has been impossible for vehicles to cross for a few days.

I got arrangements made yesterday for a car to meet him on the other side of the river. I took him down, crossed in the small boat with him, and saw him and his wife into the car. He is a lot better, but I would like investigations, before allowing him to resume work.

I hope the Tezpur plane will be able to fly today, as it is most uncomfortable to spend a night there at this time of year. There are no fans, or baths. The only place to stay is the "flat", which is a small river steamer, without an engine, and acts as a quay, owing to the variable levels of the river. There are one or two cabins on board, which provide the only reasonable accommodation. Hotels do not exist, unless you are in Calcutta, Shillong, etc. It is quite amusing to see all the floating quays against the bank at all the steamer stopping places.

Life out here goes on very much as usual. We are completely isolated, and to crown it all, one of the resistances in our wireless has burned out, and we cannot even get the News, or a song! I meant to take it to Tezpur today, but will have to make other arrangements.

I hope to have my report for the Ross Institute completed within the next two weeks. Professor Macdonald was on the list of Coronation Honours (CMG). I thought he would have received a knighthood, but he will be sure to receive this in a few years.

The tea market has improved greatly during the last few months, as have my linguistic skills. My driver keeps teaching me more and more of the language, whilst we are out in the car. He gave me the name for a metal tube the other day. The Hindi word is: "pipe", and he would not believe me when I said it was the same in English. Reita had a similar experience with the cook. He told her that the Hindi word for eggs done with milk in the frying pan is: "omelette"!

Dufflaghur Tea Estate, 1 August 1953

I went to bed with influenza last Friday night (24 July) and did not get up until Sunday (26 July). My temperature did not go above one hundred and one degrees Fahrenheit, and was normal by the Sunday morning. With the heat, however, it left me as weak as can be, and I did not strain myself to work before Wednesday.

A letter arrived on Monday (27 July), asking whether the report (Ross Institute) was complete, as they wished to get everything away to print. I had hoped to be able to write the report over the weekend, but that was not to be. The figures and tables were previously completed, and I started writing on Monday: and wrote through the night. By Tuesday, I was more of a corpse than previously. On looking at it now, however, I am very pleased with what I've written, and could not have done it better without flu.

I've had another letter from them wondering when I will be able to pay a visit to the practice of one of their medical officers in Dooars, West Bengal. I had to postpone this trip previously, but am looking forward to it at the end of August, or beginning of September. We will go via Calcutta, and Reita can get some shopping done. We need a break, in any case. This old chap (Dr Hay Arthur) in Dooars should be very interesting. He has done a lot of work on malaria control, and was doing some trials of mosquito destruction alone (DDT), without paludrine prophylaxis, this year. It will be interesting to see what his results have been.

It is a very vast subject, this business of malaria control, where the cost of materials has to be kept constantly in mind. I am trying to evolve a system just now, where I can practically point to the value of every rupee spent, and avoid extravagance. Double the amount of money could easily be spent, which would give half the results, if wrongly applied. I'm hoping that Professor Macdonald will give some financial and professional assistance, through the Ross Institute, to do a little research on some of the very potent, new, expensive antimalarial drugs in this district. I could talk about malaria for a fortnight, without repeating myself once!

Dufflaghur Tea Estate, 9 September 1953

We left for Dooars on 27 August. On the way, we were very unfortunate. I got the Land Rover over the river, by ferry, a few days before our departure, in case a last-minute flood would stop us. For a week previously, however, the electrical system started giving trouble, and I got them to give it the "once over" at the factory. On the day of our departure, the Land Rover started missing regularly in one cylinder, and I had to leave it at one of the tea gardens, and borrow the Land Rover from that garden.

We arrived safely in Tezpur, and went to the airfield. We waited up to 6 pm, and the freight plane, which had been as regular as clockwork during its weekly visits for months previously, did not arrive. When we returned the following day at 1 pm to see if it might come, the old watchman told us it had arrived fifteen minutes after we left the airfield, and had again called, and waited at 6 am that morning. We had to rush over to the official passenger airline in Tezpur itself, and went to Gauhati. From there, we took the train overnight, and eventually arrived, in a very starved and dirty state, at Dr Hay Arthur's bungalow (two days late). They had given up on us by that time, having decided that some of the rivers were uncrossable.

I visited Dr Hay Arthur's practice, and it was well worth the visit. He has a central hospital with X-ray equipment, and a great organisation, extending out to his smallest dispensary. In my practice, when a patient comes into hospital, he or she brings the husband or wife to act as attendant, and usually, half a dozen children have to be put up at the same time. This method is simply asking for a filthy state of affairs.

In Dooars, this system has been eliminated, and only the sick are allowed into hospital. He has trained some of the girls in the labour force to come in for nursing duties, and organise the hospitals on lines similar to those at home. These nurses can take a temperature, record it on the chart, give an injection, etc, and the difference can only be described as amazing.

On the way back, we flew down to Calcutta, before flying up to Assam using a different airline. In Calcutta, I discussed Dr Hay Arthur's set-up with the various Agents, and raised many other points. I hope to get a training scheme started during the coming cold weather. These schemes can meet with considerable local opposition, and Dr Hay Arthur tells me that he had to fight for his present set-up, inch by inch. However, I have managed to obtain support from Calcutta, and will push it to its fullest. I have never met a land where respect is only given by the power of your push. However, "when in Rome, do as the Romans do".

I only discussed medical services with them, and made no mention of leave in 1954. I was speaking to one of the "chief men", and he did not ask if I might be prepared to renew my contract. Do not be surprised if they give me the sack! I believe that is what they did in the past if the manager considered the medical officer wanted too much done for medical services. Fortunately, European medical officers are at a premium at the moment.

Unfortunately, our stay in Calcutta was very short. We arrived at midday on Tuesday, and had to fly up first thing on Sunday morning. We had lots of shopping to do, but I did not manage to do very much by the time I had visited the various offices, had my teeth attended to, and gone to some of the garages for spare parts: for the cars, not my teeth!

Reita's feet were swollen by the time she had gone round some of the shops, and she gave up in disgust. We did not have much of an appetite in Calcutta, due to rush, lack of sleep and over-chlorinated water. Fortunately, we had been eating like horses in Dooars. Dr and Mrs Hay Arthur were very kind to us, and the educational value was terrific.

Dufflaghur Tea Estate, 13 September 1953

I have completed my investigations for the Ross Institute, and will be seeing my report in print in the near future. I am hoping to do another survey during the cold weather of this year, and will have it completed after the New Year, when all the figures for this year are available. In this country it is possible to obtain malaria control to a very effective degree on the tea garden: probably about 90%. Unfortunately, there is always encroachment of infected mosquitoes from the uncontrolled village areas round about. It is not financially possible to do the whole area "en masse", and for that reason measures for control must always be kept active on the tea estates.

There is a certain amount of money that can be spent effectively on estates, and no increase in amount will help, unless the villages are taken into the control programme, but this is not economically possible. I have been trying to work out what aspects of control are giving a good return and require further development, and which ones could be restricted, without any deterioration in our figures.

This year promises to be the best on record, but nature has had a considerable part to play in this state of affairs. The particular mosquito, which carries malaria in Assam, would never dream of laying eggs in dirty pools, or in tin cans, as happens in parts of Africa. Most of the breeding occurs in grassy streams and clean seepage areas.

When the Monsoon broke six weeks earlier than normal this year, it washed out all the breeding places during the period when the mosquito population is usually becoming established, and this setback helped considerably in our present year's results. At the rate these ladies lay eggs, one mosquito killed in May, is worth ten thousand in August (probably).

I am hoping to concentrate on larval control methods next year, during April and May, to see if we can get the same result without the help of nature. This is interesting in that larval control has been given a very secondary place in modern malaria control. I will take this up with Professor Macdonald when he comes in the cold weather, and obtain his advice. I hope to have convincing evidence for him by then.

It is also interesting that the good results obtained this year were obtained with only half of the previous adult doses of paludrine: a saving of not far short of £1,000 in my district. Children, in whom the disease is liable to be rapidly fatal from high temperature, convulsions, etc, however, were given the previous standard dose.

The other main method is to spray the inside of houses with DDT and BHC, so that when mosquitoes come into the houses for a blood meal, they will land on the walls, and absorb a lethal dose, and die within twenty-four hours, probably in the jungle. After sucking malaria blood, it takes at least ten days, under ideal circumstances, before the mosquito can pass on the infection. The spraying does not usually prevent them from having a "bite", but if they are killed sometime within the ten days, we are quite satisfied. I could go on for weeks on this subject. It is a "bee in my bonnet", and Reita is fed up with the word: "malaria".

As I said before, Dr Hay Arthur, in the Dooars, was very interesting. His methods are worked out to the last degree, especially his laboratory facilities. I am hoping to push the point, gradually. My main difficulty is lack of staff to stem the hundreds of blood films, which are required. Dr Hay Arthur has a special man on every tea estate for this purpose: someone who is trained at his central hospital for a few months.

I forgot to tell you that I grew a beard from Coronation Day, for two months. Reita got so used to seeing me with a hairy face that she laughed solidly for an hour after I shaved it off, but she is getting used to my new appearance again.

Dufflaghur Tea Estate, 17 October 1953

Professor Macdonald and Dr Gilroy are coming to stay two nights with us, near the beginning of November. We are highly delighted, and highly honoured about this. It will be a great opportunity to obtain advice on some of our local problems. I am working on some statistics just now, and hope to have some interesting figures available for them.

It will not be long until we are due home leave. It is just over two years since we left Glasgow (14 October 1951). I do not know whether we will be returning to Assam, or not. The life out here has been very isolated, especially for Reita, who does not have her job to keep her interest alive. She says it is impossible to be interested in the home, as she was in Scotland.

I was out attending a couple (they had influenza). They had just returned from home leave, and they are being transferred to another larger tea district, for which they were very pleased. They said this was the jungliest district they had ever been in. However, if the Company have a vacancy in a better district, and the financial side is good, we will no doubt reconsider our views. If not, we will think about the oils, or the tin/copper mines in India or West Africa, where there will be a reasonable colony of European employees. I will ask Professor Macdonald about this when he comes to visit us, as he has recently returned from a tour of British concerns in West Africa.

We have been getting on with our vegetable garden this week. The gardeners planted some cabbages, cauliflower, etc, in boxes, a few weeks ago, but it is not possible to plant out anything until all the heavy rain is finished. Since then, we have been getting the peas, beans, beet, turnips, etc, into the ground, and should have the vegetable garden completed very soon. We are looking forward to vegetables on the plate.

We are able to get fish now that the turbulent waters have settled a bit, and it is a great change from the old goat. We have had a bit of beef, once or twice, but I am quite sure that they waited until it was ready to die, before they killed it.

We have not planted any potatoes in the vegetable garden this year. The last lot were like marbles, and it is not possible to get a particular variety of potato out here. It is all down to luck at the bazaar, and you are sure to get the worst at the best price.

We have a lemon tree in the back garden in a very awkward place, and Reita wanted to get rid of it, but we need the occasional lemon for soufflé. This one is too bitter for any other purpose, and we are always borrowing from one of the other managers, who has a lot of lovely ones for juice. I took a couple of cuttings today, and we planted them in another place. It remains to be seen whether these will take, before we cut the tree down.

All the hens in the labour force houses died a few weeks ago, due to chicken cholera. Our hens were very lucky, and did not pick up any infection at all. I saw an outbreak of rinderpest among cattle and buffalo, a few months ago. It was knocking the animals over, right, left and centre, and quite a fair proportion of them, especially the buffalo, died. They say that this is the world's number one disease of cattle so far as losses are concerned. I borrowed a very good book on veterinary disease a while ago and became very interested, but have not been able to follow it up owing to lack of time.

Dufflaghur Tea Estate, 23 November 1953

Life out here has been going on very much as usual. Professor Macdonald and Dr Gilroy are not coming until 7 December, now. They will be staying one night only, and leaving by the small company plane, on 8 December. The landing strip is right behind our bungalow. It is for small planes only. They will come up from one of the Tezpur practices. I have been doing a great deal of work in preparation for their visit, and hope to have some interesting facts ready by that time. I told you my report for the Ross Institute was sent away a few months ago. I have now gathered sufficient facts and conclusions for an even more comprehensive report by the beginning of 1954. This year, as well as being the healthiest, has had the lowest infant death rates on record for the practice. The cost has been considerably below that of previous years, in addition, but as I said before, nature helped considerably. I have drawn up a huge list of problems for discussion with Professor Macdonald and Dr Gilroy. Their expert advice will help me considerably to maintain the present healthy state in this district, and at the same time, reduce the cost considerably.

The weather has definitely changed now. The evenings are cold, but the sun during the day, as usual, remains fairly strong. We have had fires in the evening since the middle of November. At night, the temperature is well below sixty degrees Fahrenheit. I did not stop antimalarial activity until the night temperature fell below seventy degrees Fahrenheit: the latter half of October. Since then, the changes have been fairly abrupt. Reita feels the cold so much that she does not know what she will do when we get back home!

We are hoping to start our weekly picnics at the jungle river fairly soon. We always look forward to them, and derive a great deal of pleasure and health from them.

The temporary bridge across the big river between the two halves of my practice, was completed last week: almost a month earlier than last year. This is a great asset. We hope to have a permanent bridge by next year, or the next again.

I was reading an article in the *Monthly Review*, published by the European Association, about the new Calcutta Cemetery, opened in 1777, with quotations from Kipling and others, portraying the unhealthy conditions and early deaths from pestilence and disease. Young brides came out and died within a few months, etc. The article bored a hole into me when I considered the present healthy state of affairs relative to that which previously existed. The one main problem today is nutrition, and the wherewithal to buy food.

I have seen only one case of Blackwater Fever since I came to Assam: in a child. This was the regular menace only a few years ago. We still get the regular case of typhoid, every now and then, but fortunately, we now have the armamentarium to cope effectively with this. Even the food situation in Assam is very much better than in any other part of India.

One of the older tea planters in the district took a very slight stroke in the tea garden, last Thursday. I had to sleep in his bungalow for two nights, until I could get arrangements made to remove him by small plane. I flew with him to the Mission Hospital at Jorhat, and left him feeling fairly bright, and free from personal anxiety. He was fortunate in not having any paralysis at all. He lives by himself, as his wife and family are at home just now. It was the first time I had been in the light plane, and the view of my own bungalow from the air was very impressive.

We went to Tezpur by car today to collect some stores in preparation for Professor Macdonald's visit on 7 December. We replated the batteries on the tea garden, which meant we had to go without electricity at night for a week, and had to use paraffin lamps. Finally, my Land Rover was giving me trouble, so it got an overhaul. I have had it re-barred, so I should have trouble-free driving: at least for a while.

Dufflaghur Tea Estate, 12 December 1953

We had Professor Macdonald and Dr Gilroy with us on Monday and Tuesday. They were both very nice, and gave me a great deal of useful advice regarding malaria control. They were greatly interested in the development of medical services for the practice: a central laboratory, etc. Reita and I hope to spend a few days with Dr Gilroy during January, or February, so that I can see his laboratory, and those in some of the practices around Jorhat. My agents have asked me for definite proposals in this matter.

I am going to register for one of the DTM&H (Diploma in Tropical Medicine and Hygiene) courses. Professor Macdonald was saying that there are two courses, annually, in London. One course starts in October, and one in March. Each lasts five months. I am not too keen to come home in the winter, and would prefer to take the March one (1955).

I was doing a bit of operating today at Halem. The AMO's child, aged eighteen months, has a harelip, and I managed to put it right today. I also saw an interesting and serious obstetric case today (placenta praevia), and got the bleeding stopped. I will try to complete her delivery tomorrow. I have only had one other case like hers since I came to Assam. The previous case (about five months ago), lost so much blood in the first spurt, that I thought we would never manage to save her. Despite everything, we got her pulled round, and delivered.

The birth rate in Assam is more than twice that of Britain. One tea garden in the district succeeded in producing babies at the rate of fifty-nine for every thousand of total population during 1952. The corresponding figure at home, is seldom above eighteen. The death rate in infants in the first year of life is the same in proportion. This figure is reckoned to give an indication of the social progress of a community, adequacy of medical treatment, etc. This figure has more than halved itself since modern malaria control was initiated.

I had an amazing adventure three weeks ago. A cat, belonging to the

Halem assistant manager (who was temporarily working on a different tea estate in my district), died. From the history of the fatal illness, it was not possible to exclude the possibility of rabies, and the assistant had been handling the cat during that time. He came to tell me that it had died the previous evening, and had been buried in the back garden. We set off at once to dig it up, so that the brain could be sent to Shillong for examination. We dug it up by torchlight (quite an exhumation!), and I chopped its head off, put it into formalin, and sent it off to Shillong.

We did not take any chances, and started the course of antirabic injections. The report eventually came back that the head was in advanced stages of putrefaction when it arrived in Shillong, and it was not possible to give any report regarding the absence, or otherwise, of rabies.

Dufflaghur Tea Estate, 17 January 1954

We enjoyed the New Year celebrations at the Club (Halem). We had to have a part in the "show", which the district was laying on. Fortunately, our parts required no rehearsing, for there was no dialogue. The Club was "done up" to represent: *Puddleton in the Mud*. The *Reverend Alou Sippets* (potato crisps, when translated) introduced all the members of the Parish.

Reita was one of the three little girls from school. Of the other two, one was forty-five, and the other one was pregnant. I represented the village doctor, with a bent back, cotton wool beard and hair, a cardboard top hat, stethoscope and ear syringe hanging from braces. The "show" was very daft, but seemed to give our visitors quite a bit of amusement.

I have accepted a second contract with the Company for three years, beginning 1 November 1954. By the time we come back from leave, the first year of the contract will have been completed. I will be taking the DTM&H (London) from March 1955, for five months. The Company have agreed to give extended leave, with pay, for a total of about eight months.

Dufflaghur Tea Estate, 27 January 1954

Life, socially, has been quite nice since the New Year celebrations. Yesterday was the Republic Day holiday in India, and we went up the jungle river for a picnic. We saw the usual elephant droppings, but nothing more startling than that.

The BMA Annual General Meeting (Assam Branch) takes place between 11 and 14 February this year (Jorhat). Reita and I are hoping to fly over for about a week, and have the opportunity of visiting the various laboratories around Jorhat, so that I can draw up final proposals for one in this district. I have had official sanction to do so.

Dufflaghur Tea Estate, 7 February 1954

Life out here has been very much as usual. We go up the jungle at the weekend and try to get as much work as possible done during the week. There have been a number of dances and parties at the various clubs round about, so we have been jaunting about a bit more.

I have had word from the Agents to say that it will be in order for me to go to the Annual General Meeting of the Assam Branch of the BMA, and that I can stay on a day, or two, longer at Jorhat, to visit laboratories round about. I have already designed a new hospital for Dufflaghur, and apart from some small technical alterations, this is now off to the architects, having been accepted. It will cost between £5,000 and £10,000, plus the extras, later.

Dufflaghur Tea Estate, 17 February 1954

We enjoyed meeting the different tea garden doctors, and hearing what they had to say at the BMA AGM at Jorhat.

(Dr Gilroy, seated to the left; and Dad, standing to the right.)

We stayed at the Tocklai Experimental Station during the meeting, and flitted over to Dr Gilroy's bungalow on Monday morning. He took us round the various laboratories, and a number of the good tea garden hospitals within an area of fifty to sixty miles. It was very interesting, and gave me plenty of good ideas.

Dr Gilroy, himself, was like a breath of inspiration. He could solve all my problems in two minutes. He has done a terrific amount of research into problems affecting tropical countries, both here and Africa, when he served with the Colonial Medical Service, and was awarded the OBE. I have now got a very clear picture of what is required here. With such expert backing, it gives me a fairly free hand to get things done, otherwise I would have to go to great lengths, writing and explaining things, before anything would move.

Dufflaghur Tea Estate, 1 March 1954

I received a report from Professor Macdonald, which gave his opinion of medical conditions out here. He also said that if I kept on working the way I have been, I should be able to convert this into one of the good practices in Assam, but that I would have to start from scratch, and there was plenty work involved. I get a bit fed up at times trying to point out the obvious to people, who do not want to see, however, I have got the ball rolling, slowly, and feel quite sure that with plenty of pushing, it will continue to do so.

I have got the plans for the central laboratory completed, and these will be sent out for estimates. It is probably going to cost about £1,500 to £2,000 to get it functioning, and the Agents have accepted this, in principle.

Dr Gilroy has promised to come over, during the Monsoon, to advise me on medical matters generally. I have started preparing for the DTM&H course, next year. Last week, I started taking the book round in the car with me, and have been making steady progress. I hate to waste hours and hours each week on driving. My driver is a good chap and very honest. If he forgets to do something, he admits it, gets the row, and then gets on with the job.

Dufflaghur Tea Estate, 15 March 1954

I delivered a baby today, at two and a half pounds. We have great difficulty with our premature babies. The mothers refuse to understand that a small thing, making feeble efforts to suck, might be getting nothing. However, we strive away, and our results get better each year. Artificial feeding is not possible, unless for exceptional cases, for economic reasons.

Ten years ago, over 15% of all infants born, died within one year of birth. Even as recently as 1949, the figure was 12%. We have now managed, during 1953, to get it down to 7½%, and with our increasing effort (and facilities) hope to take it down to 5%.

The corresponding figure in Britain, varies between 1½% to 2½%. I always watch this figure closely, as it is taken to give an indication of the adequacy of medical facilities, treatment and social progress of a community.

Dufflaghur Tea Estate, 24 March 1954

We had quite a sharp earthquake tremor on Monday morning (6 am), which lasted for more than a minute. We got out of bed, and on to the front lawn, as quickly as we could, in our night attire and bare feet. Bottles were knocked off shelves, but although nothing was broken, there were some big cracks in the plaster. The whole surface of the earth kept tilting back and forward, and it looked so peculiar to see the electricity poles slanting first one way, and then the other.

Our type of earthquake is not volcanic in origin. The Himalayan Mountains are very recent in origin, relative to the likes of the Alps. As the centre of the earth is constantly shrinking, the surface crust eventually falls in slightly, and in doing so, produces a terrific shudder for hundreds of miles around the main centre. Flooding caused the main damage during the last earthquake. Rivers in the hills got blocked by landslides, and eventually broke through, and came thundering down into the valley. We are fortunate in not having any large rivers within five to six miles of the bungalow.

When we were going up to the jungle picnic place on Sunday, a female leopard crossed the road, about ten yards in front of us. She probably could not work out what we were. We eventually drove on, and left her to stare after us. Some of the keen sportsmen were saying they had never had the opportunity of meeting a leopard on that road during the day. Just as well for the leopard!

Dufflaghur Tea Estate, 16 April 1954

We have had over ten inches of rain. The grass has turned green again, and the tea bushes are throwing out leaf. The rain has kept the temperature from going up, as it normally does at this time of year. After the rain stops, it will turn hot very suddenly, and the plucking will be in full swing. They have already started manufacturing tea, but not in any great quantity.

On Tuesday and Wednesday, about 9 pm, a sudden terrific wind arose, and slammed doors and windows with its force. Many of the labourers' houses were blown over, and branches were blown off shade trees, and the same damage was done to tea bushes. The steel door between our bedroom and bathroom got completely jammed, and we had to get a man over to loosen the steel frame to get it open again.

The roads have been very bad again, and many people have been getting stuck in the fresh soil (thrown on the road to maintain height), because it did not have the time to settle before the arrival of the rain.

I always seem to be kept very busy. If my temperament were different, I could probably overlook a great deal, and jog on as many have done before me, but I am just not made that way.

The Chairman of the Assam Branch of the Indian Tea Association (ITA) came ten days ago, by light plane, to discuss hospitals in regard to Government regulations. We got quite a surprise when the plane came down, and they made their way over to the bungalow. I also had a letter from Professor Macdonald, who has returned to England. He said he hoped to see Dr Gilroy and me when we were in London, as he did not expect to visit India again for some time. Dr Gilroy has said that he will pay a visit to the practice during the present year. They are a great help in the solution of local problems.

Dufflaghur Tea Estate, 9 May 1954

I have had another spell where everything comes in at once, and I just cannot cope with it all. I also had recurrent diarrhoea for a week, but did not find any evidence of amoebic dysentery. It has almost cleared up with treatment, however, and I am now feeling absolutely fine. One is always liable to that in this land. The wife of one of the managers had amoebic dysentery a few weeks ago, and I had to organise very thorough treatment in order to get her bowel completely clear. She did not wish to go to Shillong, and her condition is now excellent.

The Agents have asked me to prepare a report, incorporating the figures in this district (malaria and general sickness), for publication (private), through the Indian Tea Association, for circulation to tea gardens in north-east India. You could have knocked me over when the letter arrived! One of the managers was quibbling about malaria policy, and I wrote a letter showing our previous results, cost, etc, and what we had to gain by accepting the expert advice of Professor Macdonald and Dr Gilroy. I will have to get Dr Gilroy to read it after preparation, so that I can get his advice. I do not get much trouble nowadays in regard to medical policy, as most of the managers are only too anxious to get the best possible results.

Dufflaghur Tea Estate, 28 May 1954

The malaria season is now firmly established. This keeps me on the run, as there is always somebody making mistakes over the control measures, or somebody trying to economise behind my back, which can be so exasperating when we have the armamentarium to keep the disease completely suppressed. However, enough said about that. Dr Gilroy of the Ross Institute is coming over for a few days, during the Monsoon, to give me his suggestions and help. This will be good for the report I am preparing for the ITA (Indian Tea Association).

Dufflaghur Tea Estate, 13 June, 1954

A telegram arrived from the Agents two days ago to ask when we wanted to arrive in England. I have said 12 February (1955) at the latest, as the course, this year, started on 22 February (1954). This will give us a wee while at home, before going to London. Reita reckons that we will be sailing on the *Caledonia*, leaving Bombay on 19 January (1955). We will have our official booking very soon now. The time should slip past very quickly.

The prices of tea, at the present moment, are beyond all expectation. I hope it will last for a wee while, as the Agents have almost agreed to build me a laboratory and supply me with some central staff for the practice. This would be a great help. I still seem to be kept very busy, and I cannot catch up with all the jobs I have undertaken.

We have had about four and a half inches of rain during the last three days, and the roads are flooded at all the weak spots. There will be plenty of trouble at the river crossing tomorrow morning. Reita is going over to stay the night with me on the other side. The mail buses have not been able to cross for three days, so we will get a big pile of mail when the water level falls.

Dufflaghur Tea Estate, 5 July 1954

We were pleased to receive your letters. When you said that June had been a cold month, we could hardly visualise it. We have been lucky with temperatures this year, except last week. The blanket of clouds, which was protecting us, cleared up, and the sun has been scorching down on us, since. I notice the heat most when I am crossing the river to the other section of the practice, and today it was very hot.

They are still talking of building a permanent bridge, and hope to start this year. That would be the best help anyone could give towards my own personal convenience in running this practice. I have started taking "tiffin" (midday meal) on the other side of the river on Mondays and Tuesdays: staying overnight simply wasted time. Last week, three buses got bogged in the sand at the river crossing when the water was high, and had to be lifted out and dragged by two elephants when the water level eventually went down, this week.

We received a letter from the Agents stating that we have been booked on the *Caledonia*, leaving Bombay on 19 January. The Anchor Line boats are two days slower than P&O, but are reputed to be much more comfortable. They take about twenty-one days. We will probably arrive in Liverpool on 8 February, and can then make our way north. At the moment I am thinking of going into "digs" in London, so that Reita can have a longer holiday with her own folks. The University (London) or Tropical School should be able to help me in this matter, unless you can get Pop persuaded to live in London for a while to make it worthwhile looking for furnished accommodation.

I have almost completed my arrangements for registration at the Tropical School, and would be pleased and grateful if Pop would send the enclosed registration form, along with a cheque for £42 to the following address: *The Financial Officer, London School of Hygiene and Tropical Medicine, Keppel Street, Gower Street, London WC1*. The cheque should be made payable to: *The London School of Hygiene and Tropical Medicine*. I would like him to pay the complete £42 now, otherwise they might not retain a place for me, and I would have to go to London before the beginning of the course to complete all the registration particulars. I will square it up with Pop when I get home. Tell him if he wants to come to London, he can bring his own blankets with him! That might encourage him.

Dufflaghur Tea Estate, 3 August 1954

We are getting it very hot just now. Until a week ago, it rained every day, and the roads are in a terrible mess. Without the Land Rover, I could not have managed to get out to work on many occasions during July. We were astonished to hear "Assam" on the BBC News a couple of days ago. The mail buses and other vehicles have not been able to cross the River Boroi for about two weeks owing to the very high level of the river, with tree trunks roaring down in the current.

When I crossed today, it had decreased to a very small river again, but sandbanks had been deposited on one side, about fifty yards wide, and they were preparing a wire, so that vehicles would be able to cross it. The sand was still soft today, and my legs were sinking up to the knees trying to cross it at some parts.

The terrific force of the Monsoon rain carries everything before it, including sand and soil. We had almost thirty inches of rain during July, and will probably have a hot August to compensate for it. There was an elephant on the river today, clearing away the ragged tree trunks to guard against possible damage to the boats. The *Ghat Babu* (ferry controller) was saying that it costs 25 rupees a day, for a big elephant to carry out this type of work.

Life goes on pretty much as usual. Dr Gilroy of the Ross Institute has promised to come over and see the practice for a few days. I hope he will manage this month before the malaria season starts to decrease.

The wife of the Indian manager of a neighbouring garden slipped on the floor and broke her ankle a few weeks ago. Fortunately, because we got two dry days, the airstrip dried out sufficiently for the small plane to land. She went over the river to Jorhat, had her X-ray and plaster applied at the Mission Hospital, and was back again within four hours. That evening, the rain came down in buckets, and the strip was useless for more than a week. They are now talking about an "all weather" strip for the area.

Dufflaghur Tea Estate, 19 September 1954

We are doing well. The worst of the heat is now behind us, but we still have the fans ticking over. We will need a fire in the evening within another three or four weeks. Reita has knitted me a pullover, and is now completing a cardigan to keep me warm. The icicles will be dangling from our noses when we arrive in Liverpool, but I do not think even that will dampen our enthusiasm.

I am now beginning to get all my business cleared up in preparation for our departure. We will need vaccination and cholera inoculation certificates, income tax clearance certificates, customs clearance, travellers' letters of credit, tickets, etc. It will not be very difficult, however, as I know exactly what is required this time, and will not be fishing about in the dark. We will probably leave the tea garden about 13 or 14 January.

Dufflaghur Tea Estate, 20 September 1954

When I was across the river today, the water level was completely down. A week ago, it was a raging torrent, and a lorry, which had got stuck on the dry sandbank, was almost completely covered. This was the fourth vehicle, during the year, to be cut off and covered by the rising level of the river. Fortunately, all were pulled out without too much difficulty.

Dufflaghur Tea Estate, 20 October 1954

Reita has started counting the days, now. I was getting a bit browned off a few weeks ago, and longed to be away, but I received a letter from Dr Gilroy to say that he would be coming over for a few days, and this has brightened me up quite considerably.

There are so many people who are not even casually interested in creating an interesting medical service for the doctor, that it is a great tonic to hear someone who is interested, and someone who is so able to advise on tricky points.

The temporary bamboo bridge over the Boroi River is now nearing completion. In a week or so, at least that difficulty will be behind me.

Dufflaghur Tea Estate, 16 November 1954

We will be leaving the tea garden in seven weeks: lovely thought! I have seen some jobs advertised in Kuwait recently in the BMJ, and sometimes think we would be better off in the "oils" where medical facilities are modern.

We will be able to go up the jungle river next weekend for the first time this season. It will be a nice change to get a swim, but the water by now will be very cold. I hope you have six hot water bottles, and half a ton of cotton wool for us, when we arrive home!!

Dufflaghur Tea Estate, 19 December 1954

We have fixed up to leave the tea garden on 11 January, and will stay a few days in Calcutta to get all our clearance certificates, etc, in order. Next Saturday will be Christmas, but we cannot work up any enthusiasm with the thought of home leave so soon.

I have been kept very busy recently with sick Europeans (dysentery), and trying to clear up all the odd jobs, which pile up at the last minute. I also had an amputation to do yesterday, and the preparation and sterility for this is very exacting. It takes much more time and energy to supervise the preparation, than it does to do the actual job. The poor patient had gangrene of foot and leg, and I had previously removed his other leg, about two years ago, for the same condition. After complete recovery, he should be able to earn a living on the tea garden making baskets, or similar.

Dr Gilroy of the Ross Institute had promised to pay a visit before we went on leave, but he had a last-minute call to South India, and will not be able to come over until after our return from home leave. I have made out the antimalarial programme estimates, week by week, for next year, in accordance with the official Ross Institute recommendations, and hope to have the best results ever recorded in the practice. This was an excellent year on half of the tea gardens, but the other half ran out of insecticide at the height of the transmission period, and spoiled the figures.

RMS Caledonia, 21 January 1955

Since Christmas, we have hardly had a minute to turn. We flew to Calcutta on 11 January by freight plane, and spent five days catching up with embarkation regulations, banking, etc. I do not know when the ship is due to dock at Liverpool. They do not like to give definite promises, but the reckoning works out about 7 February. Reita will catch the first plane to Islay to see her folks, and after seeing her on board, I will go straight to Dumbarton, which will give me almost two weeks at home before the course in London starts.

The letters ceased for six months, during Dad's time studying in London for the Diploma in Tropical Medicine and Hygiene. Contact with his parents and Mum, who had to stay on in Islay during this period because of family illness, could be made by phone.

London, 16 July 1955

Just a little note to let you know that I am getting on all right. I sat the two written papers on Wednesday, each of them, three hours: *Parasitology and Bacteriology* in the morning, and *Tropical Hygiene* in the afternoon. I sat another three-hour paper on *Tropical Medicine* on Thursday, and was very glad to get that part of the course completed.

On Friday morning, we had a three-hour practical examination in the School. They gave us a stool specimen, a malarial blood film, a section of liver from someone in the Pacific (who had died of a small microscopic liver fluke disease) and ten spot examinations of already prepared microscopic specimens of a variety of tropical conditions.

To-date, I have done quite well. When we were coming out of the School, we met Professor Macdonald, who told us that the practical and clinical examinations (which I will be doing on Monday), are the most important parts of the examination, and that no one can afford to slip up on these. For that reason, John Twomey (we met him on the *Caledonia*, and he said he was doing the same course in London) and I have been getting on with our work this weekend, as usual, so that we will not make any slips (we hope) on Monday at the Hospital for Tropical Diseases. Professor Macdonald is not an examiner this year, as he had to help out with examinations two weeks ago.

We have no examination on Tuesday, so I will take the opportunity of going over to see George Williamson & Co. On Wednesday, we have oral examinations, but I am not too worried about these. The results come out on Thursday afternoon, and I have already booked a sleeper for the 9.10 pm train on Thursday evening (21 July), and will arrive in Dumbarton on Friday. Reita wants me to go straight over to Islay, to spend a short time there, and then she will come back with me. Her father is doing very well, but gets tired at times, and wonders why he has no strength to dress himself. If Reita wants to stay longer with him, I will come back to Dumbarton myself, but I will give you all the news when I see you.

1955 DTM&H Class

Front row: Professor Macdonald (6th from right); third row: Dad (5th from right); third row: John Twomey (6th from right)

Fortunately, Dad passed all his exams. After a period in Scotland with their respective families, Dad and Mum were faced with the inevitable: the return to Assam.

Dufflaghur Tea Estate, 23 September 1955

Our flight from Glasgow to London was very pleasant with breakfast on board. By the time we finished eating, and had a smoke, we had almost reached London. The flight from London to Calcutta was also very pleasant, but a bit tiring, as we had to get out at every stop. They fed us very well. By the time we reached Karachi, and then Calcutta, the weather was very warm, and what with the lack of sleep and the heat, our appetites disappeared for a couple of days. The office car was waiting to take us to our hotel, and when I went into the office on Tuesday, they told me they had booked us for Assam, by air, on the Wednesday. We got some hurried shopping done, and left the hotel the next morning at 6 am.

On arrival at Tezpur, there was no one to meet us, as the telephone line had been knocked down between Bishnauth and Dufflaghur. Fortunately, the pilot of the tea garden plane had called in to collect a parcel, which had been taken up in the big plane from Calcutta. As he already had one passenger, he was only able to take Reita and half of our luggage, up as far as Bishnauth. It was fortuitous that there was a car standing by for a passenger who had not arrived, and I was able to hire it over to a nearby club, where a tea meeting was in progress. So, from Tezpur airport, it took me to Thakurbari Club (twelve miles away), and I was able to get lunch and a lift in the small plane, along with some folks returning from the meeting. We arrived in Dufflaghur the next day, but no sooner had I arrived back on the tea garden, when I got a letter from Calcutta, asking for a report on all the hospitals, in view of the new Act, passed by the Government of India, defining the tea garden hospital standards.

Dufflaghur Tea Estate, 17 October 1955

We have now settled in. It has been very wet since Wednesday of last week, and all the roads have been flooded. The Boroi River is uncrossable. It will be another month before the cold weather bridge over the Boroi goes up. Until then, I will have to keep on wading. Still, it keeps my feet clean??!!

This year has been a very good one from the health point of view. The malaria control programme, in particular, has gone very nicely, and this gives me quite a bit of satisfaction, after the amount of work I put into it, before we left.

Dufflaghur Tea Estate, 14 November 1955

I have been very busy this week. The temporary bridge over the Boroi River, however, is almost ready, and that should make a big difference. The weather is now very pleasant, here. This week is a festival for Hindus, and they are celebrating hard. Most of the labourers get very drunk, and the servants are all getting off to perform in the festivities.

Dufflaghur Tea Estate, 25 November 1955

The temporary Boroi Bridge, which promised to be ready so quickly this year, will be ready by tomorrow, or Monday. I have been walking over the bridge, on foot, for the last fortnight. Our garden is looking very well. We have been eating beans and radishes from it. The rice all around us is getting ripe. It is just like a field of wheat. After another week, they will be very busy getting it harvested.

Dufflaghur Tea Estate, 18 December 1955

I had a mild attack of dysentery, this week. It started on Tuesday, and lasted until yesterday, despite all the drugs I was consuming. I had one day in bed, but have not done very much this week. Reita has kept completely free of infection. The preparations for Christmas have now started. We are going to a party at the Bishnauth Club. Our own club (Halem) will be giving a party on Hogmanay, with an amateur theatrical "show" at the same time.

Dufflaghur Tea Estate, 30 December 1955

Tomorrow will be our "show" at the Club. The young fellows have been working very hard, and have produced a sort of pantomime, lasting half an hour, which should amuse everyone. The "wind", "lightning" and "thunder" effects at one part, are marvellous. The patter is also excellent, involving a "skit" at everything possible concerning tea. There is a mannequin parade of men dressed up: again, excellent dialogue.

Dufflaghur Tea Estate, 8 January 1956

We are both in good health, and have settled into our usual way again after Christmas and New Year festivities. We went up the jungle river for a picnic today. It was a great tonic to get into the open air, swimming, etc. A wild elephant crossed the river about one hundred yards downstream from the picnic area. It was a glorious sight, and not one that we get the chance to see very often.

I am in the middle of the annual musters just now. I have examined about ten thousand people, to-date: eyes of adults and spleens of children.

Dufflaghur Tea Estate, 22 January 1956

We have had a busy week. An urgent call arrived at 2.30 am on Thursday morning to go out to one of the tea gardens, about eighteen miles from here, to attend the wife of one of the assistant managers (European). She was in labour by the time I arrived (seven months of pregnancy), and it was not until 11.25 am that we got the delivery completed, and produced a baby girl of three pounds, five and a half ounces. The child was badly asphyxiated at birth, and hardly able to breathe owing to prematurity. I had to work on her for almost an hour, before we got respiration firmly established, and her colour changed from blue to a nice pink.

After that, we got cylinders of oxygen from one of the neighbouring tea gardens, to have in readiness, should the respiration again become laboured. It was fortunate we did, for the baby developed another attack of feeble respiration, lasting three-quarters of an hour in the evening, and the oxygen was, literally, life-saving.

On Friday morning we took the mother and baby to the Mission Hospital in Tezpur, by car, giving oxygen all the way. The baby took the journey very well, and it looks as if everything might be all right. This was the first time Reita has attended a confinement, and she was quite pleased to get the opportunity. Yesterday and today, we have been making up as much sleep as possible.

The record for my practice is two pounds, one and a half ounces. This was an Indian baby. The average weight at birth on a tea garden is about five pounds. Unfortunately, for every one we save, we lose quite a number of the very small ones, especially as so much depends on the knowledge of the mother.

Dufflaghur Tea Estate, 21 February 1956

Our weather has been very pleasant, and Reita took her first plunge in the jungle river on Sunday. After she got in, we could not get her to come out. The water was just lovely. It is her birthday today. She says she is twenty-one again.

The sickness rates at the hospitals are at their lowest just now. There have been a few cases of pneumonia in adults and children, however, and a lot of cuts and injuries due to the pruning and clearing up. Unfortunately, the baby I delivered died at Tezpur hospital, despite all efforts to keep her alive. She had gone down to two pounds, eight ounces, from three pounds, five and a half ounces, in three weeks.

Dufflaghur Tea Estate, 9 March 1956

Reita and I went to a "show" in one of the clubs, about one hundred and twenty miles along the bank, last weekend. On the way there, I went into the Halem post office to ask the postmaster to put a letter into the Halem mailbag. As the post office was closed, I went to his house at the back, and while speaking to him, a dog from the Halem line, kept running around and barking. The next thing I knew, it had stuck its teeth into the calf of my leg. Fortunately, I know this dog, otherwise I would have been thinking of rabies. I still gave my wound a good scrub.

I saw the dog today again, and will see it on Monday. If it is all right, then my conscience will be completely clear. A dog suffering from rabies cannot live for more than a week, but we always take ten days for safety. The children of one of the assistants at Halem, were bitten by a three-month-old puppy from the line, a couple of weeks ago. As the dog died less than a week later, it was necessary to give antirabic injections, despite the fact the dog, apparently, died of natural causes, and not hydrophobia.

Dufflaghur Tea Estate, 22 March 1956

The dog which bit me a few weeks ago, is still alive, and doing well, so I do not need to worry about developing rabies. It has never bitten anyone before, or since that time. The animals out here get quite agitated when a light-skinned person comes near them, as they are not accustomed to this. The small children sometimes get frightened, also.

The last six months appear to have flown past. The bamboo bridge is still there, but they have started preparations for a permanent steel bridge across the Boroi River. This will take some time to complete: probably about eighteen months. The mosquitoes are now making their appearance, and the antimalarial programme is under way. The results last year were satisfactory, and we are hoping to improve them even more, this year.

Dufflaghur Tea Estate, 21 April 1956

We were pleased to receive your letters and interested to hear about Professor Macdonald on TV. He is on the up-and-up, and will probably take over from Professor Macintosh, when he retires. This would make him the number one authority on public health matters in Britain. Professor Macdonald has a wide experience in tropical matters, as well as health in temperate climates.

Dufflaghur Tea Estate, 20 May 1956

The bamboo bridge over the Boroi River has been washed away, so we are now into hot weather isolation. Our cold storage is still coming up from Calcutta, by air, direct to the tea garden about twenty-five miles away. Unfortunately, on Tuesday, when it should have arrived, because of the weather, the freight plane only got as far as Gauhati, where they have radio-controlled landing arrangements. It turned back to Calcutta, and came up again on Thursday, when the weather improved: but the condition of the beef had not improved, and we had to throw it out. I hope this kind of thing does not happen too often, or we will have to go back to the old goat again: and that is not a pleasant thought.

Our vegetables are now almost finished. We only have onions, carrots, etc, left: and not many of those. We will be on to the indigenous stuff in another two, or three weeks. We had a terrific crop this year. It is the only way we can be sure of getting enough for ourselves.

Dufflaghur Tea Estate, 4 June 1956

We have just received bad news from Islay to say that Reita's father had died. He took pleurisy near the beginning of May, and was transferred to the local hospital, but despite treatment, he was not able to gather strength, and died on 21 May at 8.30 am. This has been a great shock for Reita, who was expecting him to rally, as he has always done in the past. She felt she would see him again before he died, but this was not to be. The gravestone, which he had ordered for Reita's mother, had already arrived in Islay, but he did not get a chance to see it. There was a big turnout of men at his funeral. He was well known to everyone in the village.

Dufflaghur Tea Estate, 25 June 1956

I have been very busy for the last fortnight, writing reports on tea garden facilities. Delays at the Boroi River are a constant annoyance, which is increased when there is a lot of work to do. However, there is no use grumbling. At the present moment, the *mistris* (tradesmen) are scraping the walls of the bungalow, in preparation for redecoration. This is the first touch of paint and waterproof distemper in five years; however, the bungalow should be very nice afterwards, and that raises Reita's morale enormously.

Dufflaghur Tea Estate, 14 July 1956

The weather has been very warm with the fans going full blast. Fungi are growing over the books and papers. The only contact we have with the outside world just now is through the radio and newspapers. We are going to a "show" at the Bishnauth Club on Saturday, and will be staying on the other side of the river until Monday. This should be a nice change, as we have hardly left the bungalow for ages, and this hermit-type of existence is very bad for one's psychological outlook in life.

We had a little earthquake a few nights ago, but it only lasted for a couple of minutes. The bungalow swayed gently, the roof creaked, and then the whole thing was over. Some of the sparrows, which had nested under the eaves, however, got a fright, and flew out of the nest in the dark. One of them landed on the wire mesh at the door, and looked a bit startled.

Dufflaghur Tea Estate, 24 July 1956

Mr Lunsdaine from the Calcutta office paid us a visit on Monday to discuss hospital records. They want to eliminate some of the statistical reduplication, and would like to try out a new system here, to see whether it will work, and what modifications may be required.

I do not know if I am pleased, or not, as this will no doubt involve me in extra work, and at times I have felt extra work is expected of me.

Dufflaghur Tea Estate, 9 September 1956

One of the Scottish managers was murdered on the south bank about a week ago. The labour force had been making threats for some time, and there had been a great deal of dispute on his tea garden. It was a great shock to everyone. His wife had a cousin in Falkirk, who was a patient of mine. It appears that they stabbed him repeatedly, and almost severed his head. When his wife went out into the tea garden to see what was happening, they told her that they had all taken part in it. His dog was sitting beside his body.

It is very difficult to pass judgement on this type of thing, but certainly, murder is not a twentieth century way of settling any grievance. The police have taken away about seven or eight of the ringleaders. An Indian manager on a nearby tea garden, was also murdered only a few months ago, and even the Labour Union is up in arms about it.

Dufflaghur Tea Estate, 10 October 1956

We had Dr Gilroy of the Ross Institute staying with us from Monday to Thursday, last week. He was helping with a malaria problem on one of the tea gardens, and took a look round most of the other tea gardens during his stay. He was most interesting, and also, most helpful.

Dufflaghur Tea Estate, 24 December 1956

We have a small colony of rats on the roof of the bungalow just now. They have been driven in because the rice has now been cut and cleared away. For the past few days, they have been raiding the storeroom, and chewing things up. This is the climbing black rat, which is different from the burrowing brown rat seen at home. As soon as we get the storeroom sealed up, they will probably disappear. To finish the subject of rats, I now hear of an outbreak of plague at Gauhati, which is on the south bank, about two hundred miles away: no doubt, infected rats carried up on the river steamers with the grain cargoes from Calcutta.

The next BMA meeting (1957) is at Dibrugarh, in February. We are going to fly up from Tezpur, and after the meeting, will return with Dr and Mrs Gilroy by car, spend a night at Jorhat, and then fly back to Tezpur. This will, no doubt, be our last BMA meeting in Assam.

Dufflaghur Tea Estate, 7 January 1957

The weather is very pleasant, and the evenings definitely cold. The cook gave us a present of a fish and fowl the other day, as it was the naming ceremony of his new son, delivered by me in a great hurry, a few months ago. I remember getting cross with the old midwife, and chasing her out of the room. Her ideas of obstetrics would have filled a book on "what *not* to do".

I then got a call to see the cook's cow (first baby!) in obstetrical difficulties, on Saturday. With a little help, however, she soon completed the job. I'll have to pull the cook's leg, and ask him what he is going to give me for that job!

Dufflaghur Tea Estate, 29 January 1957

Dr Gilroy is going to publish the district's malaria control figures this year. The 1956 figures have now been made up, and are the best ever recorded. On Dufflaghur, the sick rate from all causes has decreased by 40% from that of five years ago, as the result of efficient malaria control.

Dufflaghur Tea Estate, 13 February 1957

I do not know when I will be able to post this letter as the post office staffs in Assam have gone on strike for a "dearness allowance" to compensate for the high cost of living in Assam. I expect it will get dispatched very soon, and that they will get their allowance, as they are, at present, grossly underpaid. The local postmaster has the rank of assistant postmaster because the post offices are so small, and he gets about £4 to £5 a week. I found out about the strike a couple of days ago when I went in to send a telegram. He apologised profusely.

We are going to the BMA meeting this week, leaving on Friday 15 February, and returning on Wednesday 20 February. It will be nice to get away for a little change. I do not expect that we will be in Assam this time next year, but our plans for the future are very much in mid-air.

Dufflaghur Tea Estate, 23 February 1957

The BMA meeting at Panitola (near Dibrugarh) was a great success. They even elected me to the council for the ensuing year.

Dad (back row, 5th from right); Dr Gilroy (front row, 2nd from right)

The medical set-up of the tea gardens in that area is vastly superior to conditions here. They have a beautiful central hospital, with facilities to do everything. They took me into theatre to see a partial gastrectomy (removal of stomach), and the improvement in theatre techniques since I was in hospitals, ten years ago, was amazing. They even got a cataract case in to show me the operation, so that I could do some here. Cataracts are exceedingly common in India.

Dufflaghur Tea Estate, 23 March 1957

We were pleased to receive your letters, and wish to apologise for taking so long to reply. I always appear to get myself cluttered up with clerical jobs, one way or another, until I cannot see over the pile. I wrote to the Agents to say that I will not be renewing my agreement, but that we would like to stay on until March 1958. This would allow us six months leave during the good weather at home, and not in the middle of winter. I have no idea what we might be doing after that.

Mr Williamson wrote a personal letter, regretting that we would be leaving, and asking whether we might consider a practice in another area of Assam. I do not see that there would really be much difference. There are a small handful of practices where the facilities are good, but there are no openings there at the present moment.

I also had a letter from Dr Gilroy, who met Dr Hay Arthur in Calcutta. The latter expressed regret that we were going, as he had thought I would take over from him when he retired. I think, for the moment at any rate, I have had more than a sufficiency of tea gardens. Nonetheless, the malaria control programme is again in full swing.

Dr Gilroy has promised to come over for a few days, about June, to see how we are getting on. He is going to bring Mrs Gilroy with him.

Dufflaghur Tea Estate, 7 April 1957

The weather is beginning to get warmer now, and I hope the Boroi Bridge will see us through May, this year. It was washed away very early last year. I am going to see the income tax people in Tezpur quite soon. It seems I will have to get a clearance certificate from them for each year I have been working here, and that this will take months. The sooner I start, the better.

Dufflaghur Tea Estate, 28 April 1957

We are thinking about doing a trip to Japan and back while we are in this part of the world. After finishing here, we would do the trip, and then return home, preferably by large cargo ship, to get a good view of all the parts on our way home. I am going to write to the shipping agencies for particulars. My Agents in Calcutta will be able to help with arrangements. They have agreed to let me stay on until March 1958.

About a week ago, there was a very difficult maternity case at the Dufflaghur Hospital: a transverse lie, which is an insuperable obstruction to delivery, and meant mutilation of the infant. However, the mother did very nicely. A few days later, another patient was admitted with the same complaint (after hiding in the line until the last moment), but unfortunately died ten minutes after admission due to exhaustion before we could do anything for her. Today, we had a deputation at the bungalow (husband and relatives of the first woman), who insisted on washing our feet and presenting us with mutton and rice. It was a most touching and humbling ceremony to show their appreciation.

Dufflaghur Tea Estate, 18 May 1957

Dr Gilroy wrote a few days ago. He wants me to publish the malaria control results in this practice, so that it will be on permanent record. He would also like me to do some research in cooperation with him during the present rains. He says that it would create WHO interest, and should I decide to return to the Tropics (which is unlikely), it would no doubt be helpful.

Dufflaghur Tea Estate, 1 June 1957

The Boroi Bridge was washed away last Tuesday, which is exactly one month later than last year. This means the usual waiting and wading to get across on the little boat, twice a week. During May, we had rain practically every day. Last Saturday, however, it started fairly heavily: on Sunday, one and a half inches, on Monday, one and three-quarter inches, and on Tuesday, one and a quarter inch. When I was returning on the little boat on Tuesday afternoon, the river had again subsided, so that the boat stuck on a sandbank, twenty yards from this side. I had to wade up to the waist to get out of this predicament.

We have a serious outbreak of rinderpest in the locality, at the moment. I heard that a Nepali chap in the village had lost two hundred buffalo. In the tea garden, itself, every animal attacked, has died, especially the buffalo, which appear to have very little resistance to infection. The Government veterinary assistant has been doing mass inoculation of cattle, which should bring it to a halt. Unfortunately, the vaccine is so strong, that one in every two hundred of the cattle dies of the inoculation.

Dufflaghur Tea Estate, 24 June 1957

We have had a very alarming time over the last week. The Indian manager (Mr Dam) on the tea garden next to us (Bormahjan), was beaten up by a small section of the garden labour on Tuesday (18 June), and sustained a fractured skull, from which he died the following day. I took him over to Jorhat, on the other side of the river, by light plane, but it was in vain. The armed police came in force, and have arrested fifty-seven people. The tea garden has been closed from today, except for the hospital and maintenance in the factory. This is the third murder within a year, and the Authorities feel that drastic action is necessary. The tea garden will probably remain closed until the cold weather. The dispute was about the amount of hoeing that constitutes a day's work, and was not a very serious point of dispute. The manager's wife was terribly upset. She could not fly over the same day, as the plane is too small, and had to go the following day; but he had died about an hour before her arrival. The local managers are feeling very fed up with the whole affair.

I had a letter from Dr Hay Arthur in West Bengal. Reita and I paid a visit to his practice (which is a very good one, with X-rays, etc) in 1953. As he is retiring next year, he wanted me to take over his practice. He has a good air-conditioned operating theatre, with a fully qualified Indian assistant to help with the surgical work. The offer seemed very tempting, but it would still mean staying in the jungle (although not as bad as here). In any case, I have refused it, as we feel that we have had enough. Mr Dam's death has certainly removed any doubts we might have had.

We had a letter from Dr Gilroy to say that Dr O.J.S. McDonald (not Professor Macdonald), the Ross Institute representative in Ceylon, will be retiring in 1958 or 1959, and has asked for the name of a suitable man to succeed him. This is a very tempting offer, indeed. If the terms are good, we might give it a try for a year, or two. It is also a very responsible job. Dr O.J.S. McDonald's book on sanitation for rural areas is a classic. I would be a very poor substitute for him. Dr Gilroy is going to pay us a visit next month, and will be able to give us full particulars.

Dufflaghur Tea Estate, 16 July 1957

Dr and Mrs Gilroy are coming over for a few days, next week. I have started a malaria survey here, on behalf of the Ross Institute, and we will be publishing a joint report after it has been completed.

I had a letter from Professor Macdonald, giving details of the Ceylon job. It is an administrative and advisory job, and because there is no clinical work, I have turned it down, as I feel that I have not yet seen nearly enough clinical material. Professor Macdonald advised me to think hard, as it would mean a complete change of outlook. I have no idea what we will do when we leave Assam, but am not too worried. With my experience to-date, I should get a responsible job.

The neighbouring tea garden is still closed down, with the exception of essential facilities (hospital, factory maintenance, etc). The court proceedings should take place within a month. In all, eighty people have been arrested.

The Boroi River is cutting away the bank very badly at one side, this year. It carried away a huge tree, to which the telegraph line had been temporarily attached. However, the repairs will no doubt be complete in a day or two.

Dufflaghur Tea Estate, 29 July 1957

We had Dr and Mrs Gilroy from Tuesday to Friday of last week, and enjoyed their visit very much. We have already started a little bit of research in this practice on behalf of the Ross Institute. At the present moment, I am sending about one hundred and fifty blood slides to his laboratory, every week. These are for infants born this year, who could not have been infected with malaria in any previous year.

In this practice, ten years ago, the infant parasite rate was probably about 60%. To-date, however, none of the films has been positive. Afterwards, Dr Gilroy and I will publish a joint report regarding our findings. In the meantime, I am preparing a report regarding the methods used to control malaria in this practice over the last ten years and especially over the last few years.

I am quite sure of getting a job with WHO at any time, as a malariologist, but am not keen on any job that would necessitate giving up clinical work. No doubt I will end up in general practice, at home, but the practice position should be better after 1958, when some of the older practitioners, who have been hanging on to complete the ten years required for pension, might finally decide to retire.

Dufflaghur Tea Estate, 17 August 1957

The Agents are going to try to obtain a ship for us leaving Calcutta, towards the end of February 1958 for Japan. It will be a cargo ship, and because of its great number of stops on the way, it will take two and a half months to complete the return journey. After that, we hope to get a cargo ship from Calcutta to the UK.

The weather has been very hot this month because of the reduction of rainfall. Our epidemic of Asiatic influenza has just cleared up. It ran a very abrupt course for three to four weeks, and then disappeared as quickly as it came. I was in bed for two days, but soon felt all right again.

Mrs Dam, the wife of the manager who was murdered, arrived back on the tea garden for a few days, last week, to clear up her belongings. We went down to see her, and she seemed quite bright, but was rather tearful as we were leaving. She was profuse with thanks for what we had done to help.

The court action has not yet started, and I am quite pleased, because the Boroi River has been so difficult this year. The tea garden (Bormahjan) is now working normally again, but there will be a great reduction of crop because the garden was closed for a month. The growth during this period has had to be cut off and discarded, as only five to seven days' leaf is of any value to making tea with the temperatures prevailing at present. It was also too high for the women to pluck.

We are going over to Jorhat for a few days in October, in connection with the centenary of the birth of Ronald Ross, who discovered the role of the mosquito in malaria transmission: hence the Ross Institute. Our research job for the Ross Institute in this practice is doing nicely. We are following the amount of malaria transmission taking place, and Dr Gilroy will come over again in December, after the survey has been completed.

Dufflaghur Tea Estate, 8 September 1957

It will not be very long until we are on the high seas for Japan. We have a provisional booking on the *Santhia*, leaving Calcutta on 28 February. The round trip takes about two and a half months, calling at many ports, and a full ten days in Japan. Our heavy baggage can be stored in Calcutta with the Agents, until we return from Japan. We have no booking, as yet, from Calcutta to the UK, but will no doubt manage to get this fixed up in due course. We are going to Tezpur on Tuesday, and will probably not get back until Thursday.

Medical evidence for the murder case is being taken on Wednesday, 11 September. My summons to court arrived last week. It was written in Hindi script, and I had to get it translated, as I cannot read a word of script. This is the Lower Court hearing. Later, further evidence will be required at the High Court. It is a good job we did not decide to leave at the beginning of November, as the case might go on until then.

Our malaria survey is still going on smoothly. I am also preparing two other preparatory papers for publication. Dr Gilroy feels that it would be a pity not to publish the practice results over the last six years, in addition to the present survey.

Dufflaghur Tea Estate, 29 September 1957

I was at court two weeks ago, giving evidence about the murder. The eighty arrested people were jammed into the courtroom, roped and handcuffed together, so that they could hear the proceedings. As this was the Lower Court hearing, there was little cross-examination. I will have to go at a later date to give evidence at the High Court.

Dufflaghur Tea Estate, 20 October 1957

We were very pleased to receive your letters. I do not quite know what I will do when we get back home. I shall probably go into hospital for six months, with a view to the DRCOG (Diploma of the Royal College of Obstetricians and Gynaecologists). With the help of this, it should be easier to get straight into a good practice, without having to do assistantships for years on end. The DRCOG is not excessively difficult, but one must have done one year of post-graduate hospital work, of which six months must be in obstetrics. It is a much easier diploma than the MRCOG (Member of the Royal College of Obstetricians and Gynaecologists), which requires four years doing obstetrics in hospital.

Dufflaghur Tea Estate, 7 November 1957

The research job with the Ross Institute is now almost finished. The conclusion is already obvious. Apart from the stray carrier blown in, and the occasional man going out, which will always happen, at present, transmission on the tea garden is virtually nil. I will be writing this up as a report jointly with Dr Gilroy.

The journal of Tropical Hygiene has accepted a paper from me regarding the Assam influenza, which struck us about four months ago. The journal is edited by Ross Institute Headquarters in London.

I got an urgent call, late last night, to see the pharmacist on one of the tea gardens. He was returning home after visiting some friends (on his bicycle), and was attacked by two bears. We got his extensive injuries attended to last night, but his general condition is still very critical, due to shock and blood loss. If he survives today, he will probably be all right. It is about two years since we had a case of bear injuries, and these are usually very serious.

The hearing of the homicide case, at which I gave evidence, has been referred to the High Court. In all, there are sixty-two labourers still under arrest. This will mean giving further evidence when the High Court judge comes round.

Dufflaghur Tea Estate, 24 December 1957

I have just returned from Nya Gogra (twenty miles away), after seeing a case of obstructed labour, but as the patient is not yet ready, I will have to go out in the early morning to get her delivery completed.

I always seem to get a difficult maternity case at Christmas or the New Year. We are getting quite excited now at the prospect of finishing up, but I still have three papers to complete.

Each of the tea gardens is making a wooden trunk for me at the moment, to pack all our belongings for the homeward journey. It is amazing the amount of stuff one gathers as the years go past. I am expecting a summons to court any day now to give further evidence in the homicide case. It should be finished by the end of January.

Dufflaghur Tea Estate, 14 January 1958

We are now making preparations for our departure. We will be leaving the tea garden about 22 February, and sailing from Calcutta on the *Santhia* (British India Steam Navigation Co: subsidiary company of P&O), on 28 February. We will have ten days in Japan, using the ship as a hotel, and will return to Calcutta on 29 April. We are then hoping to get a freighter from Calcutta, so that there will not be too much difficulty in regard to baggage, but we have no definite confirmation of this, at present. We will probably have two weeks in Calcutta.

I had a letter from the Agents ten days ago, offering new terms if I would stay on. They suggested I take leave, as usual, and then communicate with them after I have seen how things are at home. However, I have not promised to return to Assam. I still intend going into hospital for six months to take the DRCOG: and also, to get the Assam cobwebs blown out of my hair.

Dufflaghur Tea Estate, 1 February 1958

The Agents have not, as yet, managed to get anyone to take my place. There are rumours that a locum will be appointed to begin with. We will be leaving Assam, three weeks from today. I got a summons to the Session Court to give medical evidence on 28 January, but this has been postponed. I am hoping to get this part completed next week.

We have completed our vaccinations and inoculations. I had a terrific reaction to the second TAB and Cholera, shivering violently for six to eight hours, with a temperature of one hundred and three degrees Fahrenheit. That was on Thursday. By yesterday, I was feeling much better, and today, I am quite all right.

Calcutta, 27 February 1958

Many thanks for your letters. I am sorry to have taken so long to write. With our packing, and my paper on malaria control, it has been a terrific rush. I got the paper posted on 22 February, which was the day we left the tea garden.

Before we left, we got a presentation. A silver cigarette case each, and a silver cigarette box for the table. The planters at the Club gave us an informal send-off. We have been staying at the Grand Hotel (Calcutta), and our ship sails this afternoon. We have a booking by the Scindia Line, leaving Calcutta on 9 May for the UK. It will probably take about six to seven weeks to get home. I shall write from the ship.

Santhia, 19 March 1958

We are having a very enjoyable trip, and expect to reach Hong Kong at 3.30 pm, today. Rumour has it that there are quite a few expelled Chinese on board (down below), who will go straight for Red China, and will be most carefully watched to make sure they do not stay at Hong Kong.

Rangoon, Penang and Singapore were very hot. We are now a good bit further north, again, and the weather is much cooler. The ship is rolling a bit today, for the first time during our voyage, and the wind is blowing with some rain.

By the time we get to Japan, it will definitely be warm clothes, and by the time we get back to Rangoon and Calcutta, it will be the hottest time of the year. The crew are all very nice. We have been entertained in their cabins, seen through the engine room, etc. We know the engineers particularly well, because we share the same table with them for meals.

Santhia, 9 April 1958

When we left Hong Kong on our way to Japan, we were stopped by a Chinese Nationalist war ship at 2 am. It was lying in complete darkness, and suddenly shot out a signal for our ship to stop, but since we were going pretty fast at the time, we had to circle round it to acknowledge its signal, and then we were given permission to proceed.

The holiday in Japan was really lovely, apart from the climate during the first three or four days, when it snowed. From Yokohama we did day trips, and got round quite a bit of country in the electric trams, which are just as good as the tram services at home: possibly even better.

Everyone travels by tram, and buses take secondary place as a means of transport in Japan. Car hiring is very expensive. The day we went up to Lake Chuzenji (four thousand feet), it started to snow, and not having much heavy clothing with us, we felt the cold considerably.

By the time we got back to Tokyo, the snow had turned into sleet, and we had rapidly to buy an umbrella to protect us. Fortunately, some shops in Japan stay open until 9 pm, so we had no difficulty in making our purchases. From Kobe, we did the same sort of thing, and went one day to a very famous theatre, where the "show" was really lovely.

About three-quarters of the way through, however, the "show" was stopped, and we discovered later that one of the girls had been killed in the machinery of one of the elevating floors of the stage, as she went off. We did not see anything, as the part of the stage where it happened, was below the general level. It was the first time anything like this had happened in the theatre's forty years of existence.

Calcutta, 2 May 1958

We arrived back in Calcutta on 29 April, after a most enjoyable trip. It will stand in our memories forever. It is so nice to have seen a place, when everyone talks about it. We have met several people from Assam, passing through, since we arrived. Our new ship is the *Jaladharma* (Scindia Line: an Indian shipping line), and it leaves Calcutta between 2 and 9 May. I do not know the ports of call.

Jaladharma, 13 May 1958

A few days after the *Santhia* arrived in Calcutta, the Customs discovered gold bullion, worth £30,000, on board. The ship is now practically under arrest, and as nobody will be proved responsible, in all probability, the ship will be heavily fined. She was due to sail on 9 May, but this will set her back a week, or ten days.

Our new ship, *MV Jaladharma*, is very comfortable: cabin with bathroom attached. The captain is British, but all other members of the crew are Indian. There are six passengers in addition to ourselves, two of whom, are children. After London, the ship will visit Liverpool, and then Glasgow, and we are hoping to get our nine crates of heavy baggage taken to Glasgow, which would be a great help.

At the moment, the ship has called in at Vizagapatam, which is halfway between Calcutta and Madras, to pick up manganese ore for Glasgow. Blue Funnel Line had no ship on the spot, and chartered this ship to take the ore at the last minute. We leave here tomorrow afternoon, and then on to Cochin in South India. Unfortunately, we will not be able to see Ceylon, as the ship has no cargo to, or from, Colombo. After Cochin, the only stops are Aden (six hours only), and Port Said (twelve hours only), and then on to London, about 14 June.

It was terribly hot when we were in Calcutta, and we were quite pleased to get on board the *Jaladharma*, and make our way down the Hooghly River. It is also hot here, but there is a bit of a breeze in the evening. By the time we get into the Mediterranean, the weather should be excellent.

Jaladharma, 14 May 1958

Our departure has been put back from this afternoon to tomorrow morning. We will probably reach Cochin on Sunday morning. By the time I get home, after all this time at sea, I should be able to qualify for a seaman's certificate??!! It has been very nice, and interesting to see so many parts of the world.

13

WHAT WAS GOING ON?

I'd forgotten just how suddenly and unexpectedly the letters had ended: not even a mention of the court case, although I later learned from my mother that Dad didn't have to give evidence in the end, and the accused labourers were sentenced to life imprisonment on the Andaman Islands. I also learned that following Mum and Dad's departure, a swimming pool was built on the tea estate for the use of the managers: and news of that had been most unexpected.

What was going on with Dad?

My parents' decision to leave Assam paved the way for a new way of life. Yes, Dad got his diploma in obstetrics. Yes, he and Mum had my sister, closely followed by me. Yes, Dad finally got his own practice as a GP in Kent. But somehow, the abruptness of it all felt wrong. It couldn't just end there. Dad, the intrepid medical man, who had tried to build hospitals and improve conditions, seemed to have simply given up. His earlier letters had been full of aspirations, then as the years had passed, references had become fleeting, until there had been no mention of his dreams at all.

What had happened?

14

TWO GOOD DOCTORS

Whilst reading the letters, two names kept jumping out at me: Dr Gilroy and Professor Macdonald, both from the Ross Institute. Dr Gilroy was the Principal of the India Branch of the Ross Institute and Professor Macdonald was based at the London Headquarters.

It was clear that Dad had relied very much on their help and encouragement under very difficult conditions. He had respected their advice, and diligently applied the protocols of the Ross Institute to his own malaria control programme. He'd liaised with Dr Gilroy, doing joint research with him, sending blood slides to his laboratory, and finally completed a joint report with him. All very interesting: but what exactly was the Ross Institute?

Dad had already mentioned in one of his letters that the Ross Institute had been named in memory of a British doctor (Sir Ronald Ross), who had discovered the link between the mosquito and malaria. I researched the man, and found he'd identified the malarial parasite in the gastrointestinal tract of the mosquito, proving that malaria was transmitted by mosquitoes: and he'd received the Nobel Prize for his work.

Sir Ronald Ross had been assigned to the Indian Medical Service for twenty-five years, and when he'd resigned, had joined the faculty of the Liverpool School of Tropical Medicine, continuing as Professor and Chairman of Tropical Medicine for ten years. The Ross Institute and Hospital for Tropical Medicine was established in 1926 in Putney Heath, London. Sir Ronald became Director-in-Chief until his death. The Institute later became part of the London School of Hygiene and Tropical Medicine. Interestingly, Sir Ronald Ross and Professor Macdonald had worked together, at one point, collaborating in the development of a mathematical model of mosquito-borne pathogen transmission. All very interesting.

Dad had, of course, spent five months at the London School of Hygiene and Tropical Medicine, where Professor Macdonald was based, studying for his diploma. But why did Professor Macdonald keep popping into my head? Both he and Dr Gilroy had shown an equal keenness when assisting Dad. For some reason, I kept thinking about the Professor.

I searched the Internet and found the website for the Royal Society of Tropical Medicine and Hygiene, where I discovered an article about a certain George Macdonald, Professor of Tropical Hygiene at the London School of Hygiene and Tropical Medicine and Director of the Ross Institute. It referred to him as a dominant figure in the field of tropical public health and one of the world's great authorities of malariology, and that he had distinguished himself by his work on quantitative analysis of the transmission and eradication of vector-borne tropical diseases.

The article went on to say that Professor Macdonald had died on 10 December 1967, and that in October 1968, a medal had been introduced in his memory. This medal was awarded every three years to candidates in recognition of outstanding research leading to improvement of health in tropical countries.

All very interesting, but not as fascinating as one more fact. I'd just discovered something very surprising: Professor Macdonald's first name was "George". Was this the "George" Dad had referred to in one of the interviews?

J: Your Dad's got a hat on now. He's just put a hat on. I'm finding him funny. He's just being funny. It's like a cap. Who's George?

I cast my mind back to other references to "George", and the suggestion that he might have something to do with my dad's time at university, which I'd assumed to be Glasgow University.

I'd delved through paperwork in this respect, but nothing had struck me as relevant. In light of this new evidence, I realised I'd been way off course. It was also at this time that I noticed that the person who had written the abstract for Dad's paper: *Malaria Control in a Tea Estate in Assam*, was G Macdonald.

Well, that *had* to be Professor Macdonald. But again, the question: was "George" really this eminent professor of malariology?

And then on Monday 19 November 2018 my question was answered. I had been a committee member of the Glasgow Association of Spiritualists for a year, and had chaired quite a few of the services. I was doing precisely that, one evening, and was seated on the platform, directly behind the medium, Joanne Ward.

Joanne was in the process of passing a message on to a member of the congregation, when she suddenly said: *"Who is George?"* The woman didn't know. Joanne then said: *"Macdonald?"*

I nearly fell off my seat! Of course, I took the message, conscious that the chairperson doesn't usually do that: but I didn't care. This was far too important. Joanne then proceeded to tell me that George was bringing in my dad: an academic.

They were also showing her something about Sir Arthur Conan Doyle, and were projecting an image of Sherlock Holmes carrying a huge magnifying glass. Given this project, and my job in the police, I could only conclude that Sherlock was meant to be me, and the magnifying glass was telling me to keep investigating.

When I got home, I asked my mum if she remembered Professor

Macdonald, and she said: "*Yes.*" She added that he was a lovely man. He'd come to stay with them in Assam. In fact, she'd played a trick on him. He'd been admiring what seemed to be an expensive horse ornament. Mum had told him to be very careful for it was heavy, and not to drop it. When he'd picked it up, he had dropped it, for it was as light as a feather, and turned out to be a baby's rattle. He'd found this very amusing. He'd also been well entertained by the sight of Mum, during the evenings of his visit, doing a solo performance of *The Bluebell Polka*, to the music of Jimmy Shand and his Band.

I was in business! At last, I'd identified George. The university referred to wasn't Glasgow University, but the London School of Hygiene and Tropical Medicine, all associated with the Ross Institute, and part of London University.

But that wasn't all. I went back to the photograph of the 1955 DTM&H Class and was able to study the face of Professor Macdonald (sixth from the right).

Dad had said I might have a picture of him: but it wasn't just the photograph of the man.

More digging revealed a photograph of the medal, which bore a picture of the Professor: it was definitely the same man.

(George Macdonald Medal)

What was more, I remembered the earlier references to cold heads (albeit Dad's) and the wearing of caps (Dad and George).

J: He (George) wore a cap. George wore a cap. You might have a picture of him.

C: I'll go through the stuff.

J: It's definitely George. He's got a flat cap on. But your dad's making a joke with him.

It was starting to make sense, for although I couldn't prove that the Professor had ever worn a flat cap, his photograph certainly provided evidence of a very bald head, consistent, as far as I was concerned, with a cold head, prompting the wearing of a cap. It was time to investigate further!

15

BACK TO BACTERIA

At 1040 hours, on 16 January 2019, I returned to Jacqui's. I still hadn't shown her the letters, and wasn't about to. I wanted her mind to remain a blank canvas, an ideal prop for Dad, when passing on his information. My intention was to go over previous things we'd discussed, then proceed to matters I'd researched regarding bacteria. We settled down. I got my notes out, and we began.

C: In the last interview we discussed how bacteria affected Dad's immune system, and how it triggered off Parkinson's. And we went into some detail. But I believe now, that the purpose of this investigation, is to try and establish a correlation between bacteria, the immune system and malaria. Is that right?

J: I don't think it's just that, though. I don't think it's just looking at malaria. There's how the bacteria affect your immune system with infection: not necessarily just malaria. Although I feel as though that would have been your dad's work, he's now realising that there is more to it than just that. Bacteria affected your dad greatly. For him, I feel as if it triggered different aspects of illness over the years, but it came from the original bacteria that kicked things off. I think it changed the cell anomaly in his system.

C: The following is a quote from one of the things Dad said in an

166

earlier interview:

"Bacteria is related to adaptation to the environment, and certain bacteria won't die."

J: Some antibiotics feed bacteria and try and change their molecular structure. And that doesn't always work. Sometimes you create more of an issue, and actually, the bacteria then create a hard shell that won't be defeated.

C: I think this is about what I'm just about to tell you.

J: He's jumping the gun!

C: He's jumping the gun! I found an article, dated 1999, in relation to bacteria that won't die. It's dated 1999: Henrik Wegener, Danish Veterinary Laboratory.

"New research provides the first clear evidence that using antibiotics to promote livestock growth, raises a frightening public health threat: bacteria that can't be killed. The ultimate danger is that this particular bacterium is resistant to all available drugs, and this means that it cannot be treated when it causes infections in humans."

My understanding from that is that use of too many antibiotics allows bacteria to build up a resistance: you're actually feeding the bacteria, and changing the molecular structure, which is what you said.

J: Yes.

C: And because of that, stronger antibiotics are needed if they're to fight off the bacteria. But this process simply encourages bacteria to build up even more resistance. You're changing the molecular structure again.

J: Yes.

C: So, the atomic structure of bacteria changes, and the atomic structure of antibiotics changes as well. So, everything is changing. One's trying to adapt to the other, or, outdo the other.

J: Yes. They haven't adapted antibiotics cleverly enough, like bacteria has.

C: So, the natural process of the bacteria is cleverer than man's adaptation of antibiotics?

J: Yes.

C: Nature is always cleverer than man.

16

BACTERIA AND CELLS

This was getting even more interesting: but where did I go from there? My question was soon answered. On Monday 18 February 2019, things developed further when Dad jumped in again to assist. As usual I was chairing the evening service at the Glasgow Association of Spiritualists. The medium this time was Wendy Lyon, who knew nothing about my project.

Dad stepped forward, identified himself and began to pass on information. He confirmed that when I sleep at night, he blends with me to pass on ideas, but when I awaken, I don't remember that he was there. He added that I'm doing a lot of research into something, but should bear in mind that it's not necessarily just the final answer that's important, it's also the route taken: and what I've learned along the way.

I was thrilled he'd come to speak to me: although his words now suggested that there were still plenty gaps in the jigsaw, and that I would probably have to go back and forth until each one was filled. Typically, Dad! And typically, Dad, when I found out he wasn't finished.

As the service concluded I took Wendy into the President's Room, and when I thanked her for the message, Dad popped back in.

"He's talking about cells,' she said. "For some reason he's interested in cells." And that was the start. Now Wendy, like Jacqui, does not have a scientific background, and when Dad began to discuss bacteria, she said: "I don't know what I'm talking about."

"Neither do I," I replied, "but I'm still writing it all down!" Which is exactly what I did.

For an hour, Dad passed on more information. He explained that there was still a missing link, and that it was so simple that the scientists were overlooking it. He added that they were looking too far ahead and missing the point. That they should go back to basics. This was interesting because he'd also told Jacqui that something was being overlooked. Dad continued to tell Wendy that he'd finally worked out the answer *after* going to Spirit.

And then something dawned on me. Perhaps the answer was in the medical case history that Dad was building up for himself. Perhaps he'd continued to examine it in Spirit, until he'd finally worked out the answer.

As he'd done with Jacqui, he went back to bacteria: air-borne bacteria, and bacteria on the land and in the water. He said that the water in India was contaminated with bacteria. Stagnant water was contaminated water. People drank the water. Plants absorbed contaminated water, full of bacteria, and the people ate the plants. Contaminated land produced contaminated crops and people ate the crops. The air was filled with bacteria and people breathed in the air-borne bacteria.

Dad then spoke of his own case history. He referred back to the TB he'd had as a baby, which I'd not actually discussed with him before. Mum had confirmed that. He'd breathed in bacteria, contracted TB and had been unable to breathe effectively. He said that TB had weakened and scarred his lungs. Also, because of a proneness to other chest infections as a child and young adult, his lungs were full of scar tissue. Influenza then facilitated the development of a more

170

serious illness: Parkinson's disease. Influenza is, of course, viral, but Dad's immune system and lungs had been so damaged by different strains of bacteria, that when different strains of virus attacked, they damaged his lungs further. This meant that viral infections had been opportunistic, and jumped in as well, just as soon as the immune system was weak enough.

Dad also told Wendy that I wasn't just to think along the lines of TB. Diseases such as Scarlet Fever are equally harmful to the lungs. He further said that he had had a lot of heavy colds and flus, and this was later confirmed by Mum, who added that whenever he'd been given the anti-flu jag in later life, he always contracted a very bad dose of flu. His immune system could not handle the injections, so they had to stop.

I further remembered that Dad had contracted Mastoiditis (bacterial infection) as a student, when, of course, he'd met Mum. So, what was happening to his lungs? Dad explained to Wendy that the scar tissue in his lungs was absorbing the bacteria he inhaled. He said that it was the combination of the damage already done (scar tissue) and circumstances (being in the hot climate of India) that prevented healing taking place. He then referred to humidity, stating that when the air was particularly dry in Assam he would breathe in even more bacteria. And because the temperatures were so high, his already weakened lungs couldn't heal and were finally functioning at 70% efficiency.

All very interesting: especially since he had also told Jacqui that the high temperatures in Assam had not given his immune system the time to heal. But it didn't end there.

Dad went on to talk about damaged nerve tissue. He said that because his lungs were damaged, he was not breathing properly. And because of his shallow breathing, his lungs could not send enough oxygen through his entire body (oxygen travels in red blood cells: haemoglobin). Blood was going to his vital organs, but couldn't reach peripheral areas like the hands and feet. Because these nerves were not being oxygenated, they weren't functioning properly: and that was leading to nerve damage. Dad went on to tell Wendy that dementia was linked. Interesting that he had also told Jacqui that dementia was linked to Parkinson's disease.

J: I think Parkinson's is connected to dementia. I think it's because of the nerves. The nerves stopped working: the ones that were supplying areas of the brain. I think it's all bacteria. I think you need to look at bacteria.

Dad then told Wendy that the nerve cell has to be shocked into changing its memory and go back to the way it was before: to create balance. And the way to do that is with an electric shock. Dad's case history was steadily building up, but as I went through it, I realised there was one thing I hadn't considered: psoriasis.

Psoriasis had featured predominantly in Dad's life. The disease had manifested when he hit forty: even before Parkinson's disease was diagnosed. I asked Mum about it, and she confirmed that Dad's father had also had psoriasis. So, like Parkinson's disease, the psoriasis gene was there. Dad had inherited it.

Did this also mean that after numerous bacterial infections, Dad's weakened immune system had kick-started the psoriasis? The NHS website certainly confirmed that this was a theory:

"Psoriasis occurs when skin cells are replaced more quickly than usual. It's not known exactly why this happens, but research suggests it's caused by a problem with the immune system."

It was time for another interview.

17

THE DEVIL IS IN THE DETAILS

I'd covered a lot. I'd proved who George was. I'd investigated the correlation between bacteria, the immune system and infectious disease. I'd discussed how bacteria can change itself to suit its environment, thus becoming problematic; but there had to be something else. My mind went back to the *Ten Spiritual Commandments* and the *Creed of the Spirits*, and I realised that my evidence to-date still did not explain Dad's response to mention of "the devil".

C: There is no devil.

J: Only in the details.

The matter clearly needed further exploration.

So, at 1045 hours, on Wednesday 20 Mach 2019, I set off, yet again, to Jacqui's home, equipped with notes, which she had *not* read, and recording device: fully prepared for what would turn out to be the final interview.

Before I embarked on what, or who "the devil" actually was, there were still one or two loose ends to address: and one, in particular, that still bothered me. I made this my first question.

C: Why did Dad leave India?

J: It was the right time to go. I think he'd become affected by the things that were happening there.

C: Events?

J: Yes.

C: Anything in particular?

J: Things he couldn't change. There was already a set way of doing things there. And I think some of the other ways doctors worked, not so much doctors, but the other people. You couldn't get them to work with you.

C: A bit of a lack of cooperation?

J: I think he was ready to move.

C: One thing that struck me the last time was the hygiene situation that he wasn't really able to change.

J: Yes.

C: How much of that was a contributory factor?

J: I think it was definitely a factor. You can't change what's already engrained within people.

C: I know from reading his letters that he had ambitions. Can he discuss these a bit with me?

J: Regarding his career?

C: Regarding the way he could develop things in India.

J: I think for him he wanted to create a set standard for treatment, and that was not happening, and it wasn't working, because every time he set a standard, the standards weren't being met by others. For him, you can only set a standard if everyone is willing to work together. There were problems with the medication as well.

C: What medication?

J: I don't know whether they were able to treat people with certain types of medication, but certain types of medication weren't working. I don't know whether they were underdeveloped at that point, or whether they were too potent at that point, but he felt they weren't working.

C: Was there anything in particular in that medication that wasn't doing the right thing?

J: I think it caused liver disease. It was too potent, and the liver couldn't cope with it.

C: Does Dad remember talking about the central laboratory?

J: It wasn't working. They had an issue not just with funding, but getting everything in place, and again the problem was protocol. Something to do with getting everyone up to a certain standard.

C: He makes reference to financial constraints: promises and more promises; and then the Tea Company is faced with issues and can't fund the stuff.

J: Yes.

C: Does Dad remember Dr Hay Arthur?

J: The taller man?

C: I'm not sure what height.

J: I just heard 'the taller man'.

C: Quite possibly, but I don't even know what he looked like. He had a clinical set-up in the Dooars which was very good. But he had to fight for it. He got his protocols together.

J: Was it part of a clinic?

C: It was a central hospital with X-ray equipment.

J: Like a clinic.

C: Yes. That was what Dad was aspiring to. He must have felt let down.

J: I just feel that he wishes he could have done more; but his hands were tied. And I think that at every corner he came upon something else. I don't think that they thought he would be able to change much.

C: That's sad.

J: It's really sad. But I think your dad became so frustrated, and that was why I think it was better for him to back off.

C: I'd like to read the following work reference Dad got from Dr Gilroy when he returned to the UK:

"I have been closely associated with Dr Allan Scott during the years he was Medical Officer in a tea estate practice in Assam. First and foremost, Dr Scott is a very capable practitioner who enjoys the respect of his colleagues. He has also taken a great interest in the prevention of disease and in particular, in the control of malaria. His careful investigations and supervision of the use of residual insecticides reduced a malaria morbidity rate of 60 per mille to less than 18 and this was accomplished in a district where uncontrolled rural settlements and difficult terrain make his achievements all the more impressive. Dr Scott has also taken a particular interest in accurate statistics in his large practice, and that he can make good

use of them is shown in several papers he has recently published.

I consider Dr Scott's resignation has lost us an outstanding Medical Officer. He can well be proud of the improvement in health of the large number of people for whom he was responsible."

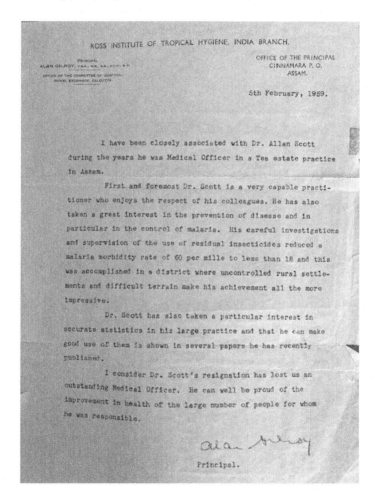

C: Does Dad have a comment to make?

J: He says it came a bit late. He finds it quite funny because if they'd have tried to make more of an effort when he was trying hard, he could have achieved much more.

C: I'm going to talk about larval control. This was one of the things that he brought up.

J: Is that to do with pupa?

C: Yes. I had a look into larval control because he wondered why it wasn't investigated more as a means of dealing with malaria. What are his views now on larval control?

J: That's still the same problem.

C: Does he feel it should be looked into more?

J: Yes, in the right way. But I think there's a problem. I don't know whether there's something they've been using with spray to try and control and that would cause side effects in humans that could go back to the liver.

C: Is he aware of other research being done into larval control?

J: I actually think that's what he started years ago. It's what they're starting to pick up on now. For years they would just spray for mosquitoes and not necessarily consider the next batch. I think they used to spray something they shouldn't spray: that would cause severe problems. Now medication has changed and it is better, but there's still an issue. It's not western society; it's over there. They're still not dealing with it. There are still problems with water issues. Water, water, water. I think it comes into a cholera thing.

C: I found that the London School of Hygiene and Tropical Medicine in collaboration with Durham University have got what they call the Cochrane review, and they're looking into larval source management. I couldn't find any other reference to larval source management in Dad's letters. Something kept attracting me to the mosquito eggs and larvae. And he's saying this is something he himself investigated.

J: Yes.

C: Did he write a paper on it?

J: No. But there's notes.

C: Are the notes destroyed?

J: Was there a fire?

C: I don't know.

J: Were any notes burned?

C: Don't know.

J: It's as if I'm trying to put the fire out. I don't know whether things were disturbed, or disrupted. I feel that I am outside. I don't know if he had a unit outside the hospital.

C: Is there no way I can get hold of the notes?

J: I wouldn't have thought so.

With nothing more to say on that subject, I decided to move on to the conversation Dad had had with Wendy. I introduced the subject of his damaged lungs.

C: Does Dad have anything to say about this?

J: It's wet lung. That's due to fluid in his body seeping into the lungs. I don't know whether he had fluid in his system and he'd ended up with some kind of pneumonia.

C: That's what he died of in the end.

J: Yes: that's the fluid that the body can't get rid of (pause) to the liver.

179

C: The liver connection.

J: It's something to do with the T-cell formation in the blood.

By this time, my lack of medical knowledge meant I was getting very confused. I decided to move on to another subject.

C: Right. Can I go back to the statement Dad made earlier regarding the devil and the details?

J: Yes.

C: My sense of what he's saying is that somewhere amongst all this information he's giving me, is the significant point. And I've got to find it.

J: I think you already have it. I don't think it's rocket science (pause); you can do whatever you want to try and fix the physical, but the soul (spirit) doesn't go.

C: The soul? No, it doesn't.

J: I think he's trying to say you exist, no matter what.

C: Whatever you do.

J: You exist. You carry on existing. Even through death.

C: And that's the thing he worked out after he went to spirit?

J: Yes. Because while he had a belief system, his understanding wasn't the same. It's only when you die you have the understanding.

C: I am. You are. We are.

J: I think the devil is in the details: and therein lies a pun in itself, because you had it from the beginning!

C: It's not specifically to do with curing the physical.

J: No. He's trying to fix the soul.

C: Ah! It's the soul he's fixing! The soul! And I was looking at fixing the physical.

J: But I think it all comes together. You had to understand him and his journey, which is why he now understands more than ever.

C: Which is why I've put a medical case history together relating to him. Is that what he was wanting me to do?

J: Yes. I actually think that the stuff to do with his time in India was good, and he's so pleased you're writing about it in a different way. And he's happy that you've gone through the facts, and who he was with, and the life that he had, and what he achieved. And he's so happy about that. But for him, he understands that his soul (pause) I actually feel as if his soul was a bit damaged from that.

C: Really?

J: In the sense that he felt and wished he could have done more. That he could have changed things (pause) that he could have made more of a stamp on things. And that's something he took back with him when he passed.

C: And if I go back to the medical side of things: what about the devastating effects on his physical body? Did that affect his soul?

J: He knew that something was wrong way before anyone else did. I don't think it so much affected his soul, because I think there were already things in his soul that were affected. He dealt with things in a different way. There are a lot of things he didn't speak about, and I don't know if that's to do with some of the people he met, who passed, people who died of illnesses, for instance, for these things did affect your father, because he was quite sensitive. He feels sensitive, otherwise he couldn't have done the job he did.

C: Does he feel his soul regressed somewhat?

J: No. I wouldn't have said regressed. These little notches are made in our soul for a reason. That's how we learn. Your dad's perspective has changed now. He can listen and talk about the journey he had in a positive way, which is why he's a healer. He's always been a healer, and if he couldn't heal, then he'd feel something was missing.

18

CONCLUSIONS AND NEW FINDINGS

So, there you had it. I'd known it all along. No Heaven, no Hell, no devil, except in the details, of course: and there had been plenty details to wade through. We create our own Heaven and Hell, and these are states we have to learn to deal with, and where necessary, overcome. It's all part of the journey of life. The reason (as surprising as this might seem) our spirits choose to have a human life. And this takes us back to our seven principles of Spiritualism.

1. The Fatherhood of God
2. The Brotherhood of Man.
3. The Communion of Spirits and the Ministry of Angels.
4. The Continuous Existence of the Human Soul.
5. Personal Responsibility.
6. Compensation and Retribution Hereafter for all the Good and Evil Deeds done on Earth.
7. Eternal Progress Open to every Human Soul.

I'd just gone full circle again. Dad had very slickly taken me to our seventh principle: Eternal Progress Open to every Human Soul. He was reinforcing the fact that the devil wasn't some kind of mystical being, but simply humankind's inability to comprehend that whatever happens, it is the soul that matters.

But was this fundamental oversight the *only* devil?

I had been considering Mum's reference to the swimming pool. That had to have been a slap in the face; and I was beginning to wonder if the devil could also be an unspoken sense of sadness that the recreational whims of a few were deemed far more important than the medical welfare of the local workforce. In other words, a total disregard for our second principle: the Brotherhood of Man.

But something else kept niggling. I was getting drawn to the pictures I'd made earlier of the spots that I'd seen in my room at night. As I pondered, I was mildly surprised when something else registered. I realised there might even be a third devil lurking quietly within the mass of information I'd been given.

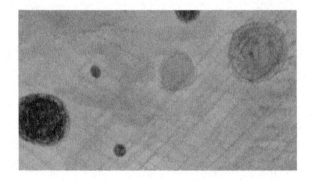

I looked at one drawing in particular: spots quivering in a haze of ectoplasm, and was at once taken back to my school days in the Science Lab: and bacteria in a Petrie dish! I found photos and for comparison purposes, was able to reproduce one as a grayscale drawing. Did this mean the spots were really bacteria?

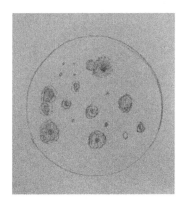

Then there were the spiders. I'd been so certain that the creatures with the legs were spiders, even after Dad had told me they were not.

C: So, who brought the spiders?

J: That's your dad as well. But I think it's just the same thing. It's maybe you just see it differently; or your eyes 'see' it differently: you're seeing them as spiders.

If the spiders were actually bacteria, then now, I got it. They *were* the same thing. Bacteria! Bacteria with legs (flagella) to help them move and spread disease.

"Floating spiders" or bacterial flagella

185

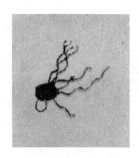

"Crawling spiders" or peritrichous flagella bacteria

I then looked at the drawing I had made of a spot emitting sparkles.

The image was almost identical to a bursting bacterial cell, which I drew for comparison purposes.

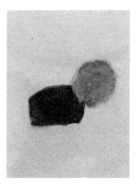

Dad was making me work again. It wasn't just about the soul and disappointment. I was going back to bacteria, the immune system and infectious disease.

But where was it all going?

Then in February 2020, COVID-19 struck. No one knew how to cure it. As the months passed by, people died, and the researchers desperately tried to find a vaccine. In November 2020, I happened upon a report in *Medical News Today*. It was by Tim Newman, and had been written on 26 June 2020:

"The authors of a recent paper ask what role gut bacteria might play in COVID-19. They outline strands of existing evidence and conclude that a link between the two is plausible, but that more research is necessary."

I remembered Dad's reference to the gut:

J: I think you need to look at bacteria: gut bacteria. Gut. It's the gut. The gut is the immune system. And you know, I'm wondering why your dad's coming up with this. I've recently had lots of thoughts about how important your gut is to being well. And I think your dad might be right.

So, what was Dad telling me now? Track down a couple of open-minded scientists, who would be prepared to take the plunge and assist me with a little more research into future and, as yet, unknown diseases? Put together a Medical Forum? Scientists, medical people and Spiritualists?

As far as I was concerned, an excellent combination: but certainly not easy. Nonetheless, possible, and maybe even the subject of another book.

FURTHER READING

A Note on "Asian" Influenza in Assam: by Allan Scott (Chief Medical Officer to a Group of Tea Estates). *Journal of Tropical Medicine and Hygiene: December 1957.*

The Infant Parasite Rate on Some Assam Tea Estates: by AB Gilroy (Principal, Ross Institute of Tropical Hygiene, India Branch) and A Scott (Medical Officer, Bishnauth Medical Association). *Indian Journal of Malariology: 3 September 1958.*

Malaria Control in a Tea Estate Practice in Assam: by Allan Scott (Principal Medical Officer). *Journal of Tropical Medicine and Hygiene: November 1958.*

Printed in Great Britain
by Amazon

61809704R00111